## THE SUMMER BIRDS

*The Summer Birds*, Penelope Farmer's first full-length novel for children, was published in 1962 when she was twenty-three years old. The idea for the book came from a short story originally included in the manuscript of *The China People*, an anthology of fantasy tales published in 1960. The story was taken out because, as Penelope said, 'It was too big an idea, too bony as a short story.'

For this new edition Penelope Farmer has, some twenty years later, taken a fresh look at the text, making subtle changes in the language whilst retaining the timeless, hypnotic atmosphere of the story.

Penelope Farmer has written several other novels, mostly for children, among them *The Magic Stone*, *Emma in Winter*, *Charlotte Sometimes* and *A Castle of Bone*. She has classified herself as a writer of introvert fantasies, concerned with 'the process of consciousness or of dream' and this is evident in much of her work, particularly in the flying episodes of *The Summer Birds* and the time-switch sequences of *Charlotte Sometimes*.

Penelope Farmer was born in Westerham, Kent in 1939 and has a twin sister with whom she 'grew up fighting, though peace has broken out since'. She took a degree in History at St Anne's College, Oxford, and in 1962 she gained a Diploma of Social Studies at the University of London's Bedford College. Since then her career has involved teaching, social work and writing.

# THE
# SUMMER
# BIRDS

## Penelope Farmer

THE BODLEY HEAD
LONDON SYDNEY
TORONTO

*To Michael*

British Library Cataloguing
in Publication Data
Farmer, Penelope
The summer birds. – Revised ed.
I. Title
823'.914[J]   PZ7
ISBN 0-370-30822-0

Copyright © Penelope Farmer 1962, 1985
Printed and bound in Finland for
The Bodley Head Ltd
9 Bow Street, London WC2E 7AL
by Werner Söderström Oy
Typeset by Keyset Composition, Colchester, Essex

*First published by Chatto & Windus Ltd 1962*
*Reprinted 1967, 1968, 1971, 1974*
*This edition, with revisions, first published*
*by The Bodley Head Ltd 1985*

PART ONE

# 1

Innumerable swallows nested in the battlements of the old house and swooped and dived all day from May to October, skimming off the green lawn surface. They were the envy of Charlotte and Emma who lived with their grandfather, Elijah, and his housekeeper, Miss Gozzling, in the turreted Victorian house called Aviary Hall, an appropriate name, it turned out. There was an enormous fan made of wide-eyed peacock's feathers in a glass case in the hall, twenty humming-birds strung on wires in a glass case in the drawing room, and upstairs a sunken marble bath, which meant that instead of climbing over the edge of a tub you stepped down into your bath like a Roman lady. This was impressive, but otherwise the house was little different from the Victorian villas you can see standing in rows anywhere with names like the Laurels or the Cedars. It had dim shrubbery, several useful greenhouses, and a large walled kitchen garden tended by a gardener called Bomble, who kept a pair of bantams under his basket chair and was Charlotte and Emma's friend.

One summer morning, Charlotte and Emma set out for school, past the lawn and the swallows skimming. 'I wish we could fly like them,' said Emma.

'And I.' Charlotte sighed. 'Though we never will,' she added. This happened every morning, but on their way down the lane between high banks buttercupped and laced with cow parsley, they met a boy nonchalantly slashing at the hedge with a stick, and this had never happened before.

'Hullo,' he said.

'Hullo,' replied Emma cheerfully.

'But I don't think we know you, do we?' said Charlottte who was always more cautious.

'No, I don't expect you do,' agreed the boy. He stood slashing at the hedge, at the frothy heads of the cow parsley, looking at them half smiling.

Charlotte nearly said briskly, 'Come on, Emma, we shall be late for school,' for he was such a strange boy and she did not think they ought to stay talking with him. But she feared it would look rude and unfriendly; besides, he was not very large and all alone in the lane on such a beautiful morning. So they stayed looking at one another, wondering what to say.

'What are you doing here?' asked Emma curiously.

'Just thinking,' replied the boy, smiling at her. 'And hitting the hedge,' he added, lifting his stick and striking the fresh green.

'Thinking,' said Emma still more curiously. 'Whatever about?' ('Don't be rude, Emma,' whispered Charlotte. 'You mustn't ask such questions.')

The boy heard and looked at her, smiling mockingly. 'I don't mind,' he said. 'What I think is not private to those who ask. I was thinking about the trees and the hedge and the morning and about that lark thrown high up there in the sky. And now I'm thinking about you. I like thinking.'

Emma was impatient. 'You'll be late for school if you stay here thinking much longer,' she cried.

'I?' said the boy. 'I don't go to school.'

In surprise Charlotte said, 'Oh, but I thought everyone had to go to school,' while Emma jumped up and down on her short legs and shrieked, 'Come with us, come with us, why don't you come with us?'

But Charlotte looked at him doubtfully. He had a freckled, winged face with wide slant eyes of a brown that was almost red, like chestnuts. He wore a faded blue shirt, speckled like a thrush's egg, above patched leather shorts, and his legs were long and bare, brown as an Indian's. He was remote and wild. She could not explain or understand him; so she said cautiously, looking at the red lighting of his eyes, 'I don't know what our teacher would say.'

But Emma was never cautious. 'Do come,' she pleaded.

He stood silent there, watching them. Then he raised his head and looked up at the lofty sky. In the silence they could hear the shrill shouting of the lark, and suddenly they saw it high above them, in the blue; a bird, a glint of goldfinch, darted in eager flight from the hedge, skimmed over their heads, and was gone. At that the boy gave one last sharp blow at the bank with his stick, making the grasses quiver, and turned to Charlotte and Emma. 'Yes, I will come with you,' he said, and throwing the stick deliberately from him, set off at such a swift pace down the hill that they had almost to run to keep up with him. He said not another word.

# 2

Although it was nearly nine o'clock when they reached the school gates, the children were still playing in the yard like so many earth-bound sparrows, chattering and calling, the girls on the left side with skipping ropes and the boys with a football on the right. It was only a small yard. Quite often the skipping and the football entangled, and the boys would shout at the girls while the girls shrieked at the boys for interrupting.

When Ginger Apple saw the sisters, he came running over, followed reluctantly by Totty Feather who did not like girls but had to put up with them because Ginger was his friend and Ginger loved Emma. Charlotte wondered what they would think of the strange boy, but they did not seem to notice him. She tried to introduce them as her grandfather would, saying, 'Ginger, I don't think you know. . .' and then stopping because she suddenly remembered that she did not know the boy's name. But the two boys, Ginger and Totty, looked at her as though she were talking of ghosts. Ginger was shy and redheaded and heavy, and when he blushed as he did before Emma, the colour of his face clashed with his hair.

'H-h-hullo, Em,' he said. 'Hullo, Charlotte.'

'Hullo, Ginger; hullo, Totty,' Charlotte answered.

Emma, uninterested, giggled and said, 'You're blushing, Ginger,' and ran across the yard calling her friends. 'Annie! Marly! Molly! Can I play too?' Charlotte was left with the strange boy behind her and Ginger in front, wondering how to comfort poor heavy Ginger, who was redder than ever with sadness because Emma had rushed away. He, and everyone else in the school, thought Charlotte was a prig. None of them knew how difficult it was for her living between Emma, who was always naughty, and their grandfather, who liked little girls good. So Charlotte stood shy, and Ginger stood blushing by the big school gates, while Totty Feather waited for Ginger, plucking at his sleeve. The boy behind surveyed them with an odd half-smile.

At that moment, Miss Hallibutt, the teacher, came out ringing the big brass bell. The shouting and chattering changed from skipping and football shouts to school-morning ones such as, 'It's my turn to collect books today, so just you mind out, Molly Scobb!' as the children streamed out of the sunlit morning into the schoolroom.

'Silence, children, silence!' fussed Miss Hallibutt distractedly behind them, her hair falling down. 'Silence, silence,' and gradually their whisperings died away altogether, and the banging of desk lids ceased.

The boy had followed Charlotte into the schoolroom. But no one seemed to notice him, no one nudged Charlotte and said, 'Who's that?' in a loud whisper, as they usually did with strangers; indeed it was almost as if they did not notice him at all. He sat cross-legged on the floor between Charlotte and the window, watching Miss Hallibutt open the attendance book with its scarlet binding and survey her class. Miss Hallibutt looked straight at him, but she did not say, 'I was not aware that we were to have a new pupil,' or some such remark. It seemed that her pebble-grey eyes, staring at his thin body, saw only air.

But she looked round at all the other children sitting

11

two by two in her classroom, with its maps and its ink stains, with its jar of buttercups drooping on the high window sill beside the window cord, the yellow petals falling on the floor in a dust of pollen.

'John Apple,' she said.

'Here, Miss,' answered Ginger in his funny hoarse voice.

'Thomas Feather?'

'Here,' cried spectacled Totty quickly.

'Robert Fumpkins?'

'I'm here,' said Baby importantly because his parents owned the only television set in the village.

'William Scragg?'

'Here,' said Bandy, the butcher's son, with his wicked sideways grin.

'George Dimple?'

'Here,' replied Scooter, trying to sound wicked like Bandy but only sounding solemn.

'James Hat?'

'I'm here,' shrieked eager Jammy, the smallest in the class.

'Annie Feather?' asked Miss Hallibutt, turning to the girls.

'Here,' said Totty's sister, heavy and serious.

'Molly Scobb?' She was Annie's best friend and wore a pink hair ribbon.

'Here,' she said.

'Marlene Scragg?'

'Here,' declared Marly, looking almost as wicked as her twin brother Bandy with the same sideways grin.

'Magdalen Hobbin?'

'Here,' answered the remote brown-legged girl they had nicknamed Maggot. She lived with her gamekeeper uncle in a cottage in the woods. He took little notice of her, and no one knew what had happened to her parents.

'Charlotte Makepeace?'

'Here,' said Charlotte, wondering about the strange Maggot as she always did.

'And Emma Makepeace?'

'Here, I'm here,' cried Emma last of all.

As the morning went on, Charlotte's attention wavered from the lessons; she watched shadows on the ceiling or a careless fly buzzing on the window or the falling buttercups, instead of reading the words in the books.

The boy grew increasingly impatient.

'Why are we waiting?' he whispered to her at last. 'Won't you come on?'

'But where?' hushed Charlotte bewilderedly. 'How can I come? It's schooltime. I shall be missed.'

He looked scornfully round the classroom. It had grown hotter during the morning. The heat swelled among the desks crowded together, in and out of the sleepy-backed children. The only live thing was the sunlight, which burned on the floor by the window and picked out the colours of the dresses and the lights in the children's hair. Even the teacher's hand moved more slowly over the blackboard, and the silence was as thick as velvet.

'Come on,' said the boy again. 'I can teach you more than this. Come on, come on, come on, before I burst!'

Charlotte, still bewildered, found herself sitting with him on the windowsill, and a moment later they had jumped out onto the grass beneath the window. They landed in a heap like puppies and sat up smiling at each other. Charlotte was surprised to find that she did not feel in the least guilty at playing truant. All that mattered was that it was a beautiful morning and she was out in it and happy as a bird.

# 3

The boy seized her hand again and pulled her to her feet.

'Come on,' he cried joyfully. 'I feel alive again. It was a death in there, chalk, ink, paper death. How could you bear it? I want to run now till I've no breath left.'

They ran over the grass of the meadow between the sun and the buttercups, the cool breeze on their foreheads, easy as deer. Charlotte, holding tight to his hand, thought she had never gone so fast. The close heat of the classroom was no more. She felt only freedom and air, and laughed to run, her hair streaming behind. Perhaps this was how swallows felt, skimmering over the lawn.

They flung themselves down at last under the trees, panting, to regain their breath. Charlotte lay flat on her tummy and felt the soft grass on her face and an insect wandering over her legs. The boy was silent for a while, wondering about something, it seemed to Charlotte, who turned her head sideways to watch him.

'Would you like to fly?' he asked suddenly, sitting up and hugging his knees.

Charlotte felt a flicker of excitement, but knowing that such things did not happen in an ordinary world, she only said practically, 'What, in an aeroplane? No, I don't think perhaps I would. I should be so frightened. Why? Have you got one?'

'No, goose,' said the boy, mocking again. 'I mean fly as a bird. I can teach you if you want.'

Round-eyed, Charlotte still dared not believe him. She

14

sat up on her knees and looked at him.

'But how can I fly?' she said. 'It's impossible; only birds can fly.'

'Nonsense,' he answered her scornfully, 'nonsense, nonsense! Watch me!'

He leaped gracefully, easily into the air, circled Charlotte, laughing at her astonishment, and came softly to the ground in front of her. 'See, doubter?' he said. 'Now watch.'

Before she could overcome her surprise, she found herself performing, under his instruction, a whole string of exercises to develop her flying technique and make her accustomed to the movement. She had to push her arms as though she were swimming, do knee bends to strengthen her leg muscles, circle her wrists and ankles so that they would be supple and easy for the flying action. When she had done each of these in turn, she had to do all of them together, lying on her stomach in the grass and practising till she was breathless and exhausted. She found it nearly impossible, like trying to beat out a different musical rhythm with each hand at the same time. But at last the boy seemed satisfied and had her climb onto a fallen tree trunk and jump from there, using her arms and legs as he had shown her. She landed with a jarring bump on the grass. The boy showed her again patiently, no longer mocking. He hovered in the air and came quite slowly to the ground.

Charlotte tried once more, but this time nearly twisted her ankle. The boy was relentless, more relentless than Miss Hallibutt.

'Try again,' he said. 'Try again. The knack will come.'

But although she was trying very hard, the knack seemed slow to reach her. She felt like a baby thrush first learning to fly, flopping off a branch without wind in its wings. Then Charlotte found herself staying in the air for a while. At the first realization she was so alarmed that she fell to the ground again with a bump.

Yet slowly she became used to the feeling of flight, as a learning skater grows to skates. She became bolder, and the boy decided that she was ready to fly properly. She climbed with him up the nearest tree, up and up, the rough bark scraping her hands, the wood living and moving under her feet, up and up, the leaves brushing her face, till they swayed precariously on the highest branch that would bear their weight.

The ground seemed a world away, swaying and receding between the leaves of the tree. Twig on twig, branch on branch, gold and green beneath them mingled with the same sunlight, which caught her on the side of the head and splashed the boy's shirt. She could feel the warmth of it on her hair; the purr of wood pigeons filled her ears, and she was more frightened than she had been in the whole of her life. But she was determined not to show it before the boy's mocking smile, so she shut her eyes, clutched the rough wood, and waited.

'No stop till we reach the oak tree,' he whispered. 'Are you ready? Now jump! jump!' Somehow she had left the living, swaying tree. The leaves touched her face. She brushed through them and came out into the full glare of the open meadow, twenty feet above the ground. She was flying. But it was not easy, as birds seem. She was flying, yet still the right rhythm would not come. For a second it was there: she swooped delightfully over the grass, and in a flash it had gone and she was left struggling in mid-air, leg-arm moving one after the other like a swimmer in difficulties. By the time the tree was only a few yards behind them she was exhausted, envious of swallows. She ached all over and her breath came in gasps.

'I can't do it,' she gasped out.

'Of course you can, goose,' cried the boy, hovering easily and laughing at her struggles, but not unkindly. 'Push together; move your ankles more, and your arms. Don't flap wildly like a worried hen: together.'

And quite suddenly she understood. Her movement ceased to be choppy and hurried like a frightened swimmer, but slowed to an easy acceptance of rhythm, the pull of the arms, the turn of the ankles: in, out, together. Soon she was sitting jubilant on the branch of an oak tree, eager for more. She shut her eyes and jumped out again into the sunlight. For one terrible moment she thought she had lost the knack; she was struggling, flapping; yet suddenly it was there again, the wholeness, the lightness of movement. She skimmed over the meadow, wind-soaked, with the ease of swallows.

She wondered how she could have thought that running was like a swallow flying. This was different, extraordinary, ecstatic. Yet still she could not make a swallow's angled swoop, skim up and away, sudden to turn. The boy showed her, but when she tried, she nearly landed on her nose in the grass; so she stayed level in flight, and whenever she had to descend or ascend, she went slowly, with care.

'Well done, Charlotte!' The boy shouted approval beside her. 'Well done. You'll not forget it now.'

But it was tiring all the same, and she was glad when they collapsed at last in the long grass at the far corner of the meadow and lay there panting, the fronds of grass waving above them and the shrill grasshoppers all round.

# 4

Charlotte laid her head wearily on the ground and hugged her joy to herself. The boy rolled over on his stomach and surveyed her, chewing a piece of grass. Suddenly, he reached over and tickled the back of her neck. Absorbed in her own world, she jumped.

'Goodness, you frightened me,' she said.

The boy laughed. 'Good.' He grinned broadly at her then. 'I've had my patience tried this morning. What a slowcoach you were learning. But you tried well enough. I like you.'

'Thank you—that's so kind of you,' said Charlotte, trying to joke, but desperately pleased inside because so many people thought her a prig. She buried her head in the grass, feeling her face scarlet, and would not look at him.

'Do you know many people, Charlotte?'

Charlotte, trying to look as though it were her own choice, said, 'No, I don't. Do you?'

'No,' said the boy abruptly. They lay in silence for a little while, their eyes closed, in the heat and warm-grass smell of summer.

'Tell me about you, Charlotte,' the boy started again suddenly. 'Where you live, what you do. I want to know.'

Charlotte at first did not know how to begin; she wanted to be angry at his curiosity. But suddenly she found herself, with great enjoyment, telling him about their house with its turrets, and their grandfather who liked little girls good and Emma who liked being naughty, and about herself who was very bad at persuading their grandfather that naughty little girls could be nice and Emma that being good wasn't always impossible. She told him about the housekeeper, Miss Gozzling, who tried to be strict but who was too old and lazy, and Bomble who was old and lazy, too, but very kind and who taught them to make paper boats to sail on his water tank, and about the greenhouses, which were warm and smelled of tomatoes and about the Roman bath, which you stepped down into; and about the peacock-fan and the humming-birds and the swallows, particularly about the swallows.

'You must come to tea and see it one day,' she said, excited. 'Would you like to come? Do come, please.' It was only then that she realized that she knew nothing about the boy or where he came from, or even what his name was, and that usually you only asked to tea people you knew and whom grown-ups considered respectable. But of him she knew nothing at all. So she grew stiff and shy again and said politely, mustering all her courage, 'But you must tell me your name, please, and where you live. Grandpa is sure to ask.'

The boy who had been listening to her interestedly without mockery now smiled the strange, frightening smile that lit his chestnut eyes. 'Quizzy monkey!' he said, raising his right eyebrow at her. 'What does that matter to you. I'm here, that's all.'

Charlotte blushed, thinking perhaps she had hurt him. Perhaps he was an orphan, and you didn't ask orphans about their homes. So she fell silent and did not know what to say.

When she looked at him, however, there was no sad orphan look on his face; there was only a mischievous

19

glint, a half-smile, as though he were enjoying being mysterious. A few hours before she would have been suspicious and worried. But now she was sure that strange as he was, there was no need to fear him and that it was no use asking him questions. One day, maybe, he would tire of secretiveness and tell her of himself. As for now, it was summer, she had learned to fly, she had a new friend, and nothing else mattered. So she lay on her back with her head on her hands and watched some small clouds sailing across the sky.

'And the school—the other children?' asked the boy suddenly, watching her while his fingers carefully unthreaded the seeds from a stem of grass. 'Would they like to fly?'

Charlotte did not know them very well, but she said, 'I'm sure they would like flying as much as me.'

'Would they?' said the boy. His face lit up. 'Would they like to learn to fly too, and could we go on flying picnics, you and I and all of them, as a band, together?'

Charlotte grew excited too, even though part of her wanted to keep the boy all to herself. 'Yes, yes,' she cried. 'Couldn't I help you teach them to fly too—one Saturday here in the field?'

The boy laughed at her, but more kindly this time. 'No,' he said. 'It cannot be—only one by one, a new pupil each day. That's all I can manage.' Then he looked at her, raising an eyebrow and smiling his strange, secret smile. 'It's a secret,' he said. 'No telling. And I'll come to tea with you one day.'

They lay silent in the grass for a little longer. But the sun was high in the sky and it seemed near lunchtime, so the boy leaped to his feet and pulled Charlotte to hers.

When she jumped from the windowsill, where buttercups were drying in a glass jar, down into the hot, chalky

20

schoolroom, the boy had gone without her realizing it. No one seemed to notice her come back; no one seemed even to have noticed she had gone. The teacher's hand moved slowly over the blackboard; the clock hands crept slowly towards half past twelve. Charlotte wondered panic-stricken if she had only been dreaming. But the bell rang at last. When they ran out into the little yard for lunch, she found that the smallest kick still sent her soaring into the air, and she had to come hastily to the ground again, terrified lest anyone should see her. Hugging her secret, she did not mind when Molly Scobb ran past, her pink hair ribbon undone, and cried, 'Mind out, Miss Prig!'

Emma was suspicious. She had not seen Charlotte go or come back, but she wondered about the boy and what had happened to him. And she noticed Charlotte's untidy hair, the ribbon slipping off, in place of her usual neatness, noticed her shining eyes and sunburned cheeks. She had never seen Charlotte look like that before.

'You've got a secret, Char. I know you have. Tell me, tell me—please. I promise I won't tell anyone else,' she pleaded on their way home at four o'clock. 'I'm ten, after all; I can keep a secret—you know I can, Char. Please, won't you tell me?'

Charlotte said, 'But I haven't, Emma,' and tried to look normal, though she did not feel it.

'Pig, pig, pig, beastly pig, I know you have a secret,' cried Emma, pink in the face. 'You're the horridest person on this earth and I hate you!' And she ran ahead all the way up the lane. Charlotte was sorry and longed to tell her. But even when they passed the swallows on the lawn and Emma, her temper recovered, said wistfully, 'Look at them; I wish we could fly too,' even then

Charlotte remembered her promise and kept the secret inside her. A flying school! And soon Emma would know, too. Soon all of them would know, all the children together, and they would fly, a school of swallows, skimming, diving, a flight of children.

# 5

The next morning Emma, who was vain, wore her best blue-checked gingham dress, in which someone had once told her she looked sweet, and brushed her dark curly hair till it crackled. Charlotte guessed Emma was jealous of her because of the secret she suspected and was hoping that the boy would be there again. When Emma saw Charlotte looking at her, she said sweetly, 'Please, Charlie, will you tie my hair ribbon for me?' and giggled all the way through breakfast while their grandfather Elijah read his newspaper. Once he even looked up, peering round the pages, over the pot of Oxford marmalade and the bulbous toast rack, over their silver mugs, towards Emma, to say, frowning, 'That's quite enough of that,' in a warning way, his grey eyebrows drawn together. But still Emma giggled, though more quietly, while Charlotte, growing cross, kicked her warningly under the table and watched the quivering of the voluminous pages of *The Times* behind which their grandfather was hidden.

After breakfast they set out once more down the drive, their satchels bumping on their backs. The swallows flew high again, which meant that the day would be fine. Already it was a joyful, many-coloured morning that should not be spent in a chalk-filled classroom, thought Charlotte, unusually resentful.

Once more the boy was standing in the lane by the hedge. He looked up at them as they came towards him.

'Here again,' he said disinterestedly. His stick moved continuously among the grasses.

'Hullo,' answered Emma crossly, because yesterday he had gone with Charlotte.

The boy laughed at her mockingly. 'Don't be such a crosspatch,' he said. 'It's much too good a morning, isn't it, Charlotte?'

'Yes, it is,' said Charlotte stiffly, though yesterday she had known him so well. Since yesterday she had thought of little but him and flying. Yet, faced again with his mocking eyes, she looked at her feet, scuffing a pebble into the road edge under the overhanging grasses, and did not know what to say. She could feel herself blushing and hated her own stupidity.

Emma giggled at her. 'Charlie's blushing,' she said heartlessly. Charlotte looked into the air, into the sun-filled sky, rather than look at the boy. She was sad because she knew that today he would go with Emma, and because she thought he laughed at her.

But he only said, 'Cheer up! Two crosspatches on such a morning! Come on or we shall be late!'

Emma chattered all the way down to the school, her crossness over, but Charlotte watched the boy and saw his strangeness far more clearly than she had done the day before when knowing him was new. How like a bird he was, the way his nose sprang out from his face like a beak, his bright, straight eyes, even his walk, springy, half-ungainly, half-graceful, the jerky step of a long-legged bird. The freckles on his nose were not haphazardly scattered as most people's are. It came to her that they made a cockleshell on his face, the top at the bridge of his nose, the span of it stretching out equally over his cheeks on either side.

She pondered, too, an action of his, a sudden snatch

24

with the hand, from the air to his mouth, or else a swift thrust of his head, the mouth open and immediately snapped shut. She noticed it again now and thought it like a bird, an insect-catching bird, and in proof saw the glint of an insect in the hand that went swift to his mouth.

'Do you eat insects?' she burst out, horrified, forgetting her silent shyness.

'Of course, it's my breakfast, and I'm hungry,' he answered, mocking her horror. 'You should try them; they're tasty bites. Bees are best, but you have to be careful not to eat the stings. Grasshoppers are good too.'

She could scarcely believe it and looked at him wide-eyed in wonder, while Emma skipped in the lane and cried, 'Do you really? Will you teach me too?' and plagued him with all the questions Charlotte dared not ask.

But he refused to answer.

Inside the school gates it happened. When Emma ran off to find her friends, the boy went loping after her and left Charlotte sad and alone. She walked slowly and miserably across the yard to where Maggot Hobbin was skipping by herself, away from the other girls. They liked each other, these two, Charlotte Makepeace and Maggot Hobbin, though neither ever said much to the other. Charlotte, indeed, did not understand Maggot at all, though Maggot seemed to know most things about her, for she had a strange wise way of looking at people that made her seem omniscient. Now she just said hullo to Charlotte, very briefly, and went on skipping, to finish the figure she had started, her long dark hair whipped scarum round her face. That done, she handed one end of the rope to Charlotte, and they skipped in unison, a jumping pair—quiet in the yard full of chatter like starlings'. But all the time Charlotte was watching the boy unseen behind Emma, who shouted with Annie and Molly in a corner.

Jammy Hat came running over to Maggot as they were skipping, his knee skinned. He was trying to hold back the tears, which pushed from his eyelids at the pain. He was a little round, bouncy boy, and he did not want to shame himself in front of the big boys; but he would not run in his smallness to the other mothering girls. Maggot, who never treated him as a little child, found a grubby handkerchief and gravely bound up the knee for him. She smiled her shy, wild smile, and he ran off happy again to join the others.

'Poor Jammy,' said Charlotte, smiling because he was so small and feeling motherly towards him.

'No, he's all right,' said Maggot severely, then she said, 'How did you meet him?' indicating Emma with her head.

'Oh!' cried Charlotte in surprise. 'I thought nobody could see him except us.'

'But I can,' said Maggot. 'My great uncle taught me such things,' she added. But she saw Charlotte's reluctance and asked no more.

In school, when Charlotte looked up halfway through the second lesson, the boy and Emma were gone. How hot, how stifling, how aching hot it was; how she wished she could go too. But she could only sit bowed over her arithmetic book. As if to increase her longing, she suddenly heard Emma's laugh from the meadow. And in the sky a long way off what seemed to be a huge bird rose briefly and then was gone.

# 6

At the end of the morning, Charlotte thought suddenly with fear, 'Emma isn't back,' but then she saw her at the other side of the classroom, eyes shining, obviously bursting to talk, yet silent. She seemed to be waiting for Charlotte, which was strange, because most days she rushed out with Molly and Annie and Marly. 'I didn't even hear her come back,' thought Charlotte with surprise. 'I wonder when she came.' And suddenly she was longing to talk to Emma, to compare their flyings.

'Charlie!' said Emma as they got out of the door.

'Emma!' said Charlotte at the same instant. They looked at each other, words held for a moment from tumbling out.

'Can you?' said Charlotte. 'Did he?'

'And you?' said Emma.

'Yes—fly!' they both shouted together and rushed across the yard madly, Charlotte's jealousy gone in the sudden memory of flight and the joy that she need have no secret from Emma any more.

'Isn't it *super*,' said Emma, no longer wordless as they sat down by the railings where the chestnuts thrust lanterned branches over their heads into the yard. 'He said I learned quickest of anyone he's ever taught,' said Emma, 'and we went for a fly around, and we talked about you, and he told me lots of things about birds, and he made me eat a grasshopper but I didn't like it very much, and he was horrid and I got angry—sometimes

27

he's a horrid boy—and he said I was being silly and I wasn't; it was horrid. But, Charlie, isn't it super?' she cried in almost one breath.

'Yes, yes, yes!' cried Charlotte, excited too, though she was slightly annoyed inside herself that Emma had learned so quickly and wondered what they had been saying about her.

'Isn't it funny the way he can be invisible and make us seem so too?' Emma rushed on. 'He says it's something he's got inside him, and he can't teach us, but it's very useful.'

'Maggot Hobbin can see him,' Charlotte was about to add, but caught the words in time. She had better be silent about Maggot because she did not understand her, so she merely said gravely, 'It's very useful.' She looked at Emma's glowing face and laughed, but wished she had been able to talk to the boy as easily as Emma. She hated her jealousy, but it came despite her.

'Hullo, Charlotte, hullo, Chatterbox,' said a voice. It was the boy standing behind them.

'Your sister,' said the boy firmly. 'I'll report on her; a quick learner, but she talks too much and her temper is unsteady; not a nice, obedient pupil like her sister.' He grinned broadly at Charlotte with birdlike eyes, his cockleshell freckles very pronounced, and suddenly she was no longer jealous of Emma.

'Would you like some lunch?' she asked, smiling at him and thrusting out their sandwiches. She was filled with remorse at her disgust of his insect-eating in the morning. It was probably because he was hungry, poor boy, and she had never thought that he might be or offered to get him some food.

The boy hesitated. Then he said, 'No thank you,' looking at her. 'There won't be enough for you. No,

28

don't worry, Charlotte; I am fond of insects. To me they taste as milk and honey to you, and I have already eaten many today.' Charlotte who had never eaten milk and honey looked doubtful, but the boy would take nothing. He stayed talking till suddenly there was only his voice behind them mocking. 'See you tomorrow, sisters!'

They sat in silence under the chestnut trees, eating, their thoughts elsewhere. They felt apart from the school noises, the chatterings and callings, quarrellings and questionings. They were closer to the purr of pigeons and the murmur of chestnut leaves above their heads. The school bell's clanging disturbed from another world. Sighing, they rose to their feet and brushed off the crumbs, while Charlotte folded the sandwich papers. Then they walked in, ready to sit through another dragging afternoon.

But at last it ended. Charlotte and Emma came out of the classroom and quickly said goodbye to their friends. As they went through the yard, they heard solid Annie and pink-ribboned Molly whispering that Emma Makepeace was very stuck-up all of a sudden, what could have come over her? She was getting just like her sister, prig Charlotte, all standoffish. Emma stuck out her tongue at them and said, 'Just you wait, Annie Feather,' furiously. But Marly Scragg, careless and uncaring as her brother Bandy, grinned broadly at them as she went by, leggy and sharp-angled as a boy.

# 7

Charlotte wondered if Emma would give them away by her impatience. She jigged excitedly, but except for one or two suspiciously soaring jumps, she managed to hold herself till they turned the corner up the dusty lane and the high hedges hid them from sight. Then she sprang into the air, and Charlotte, fearful that her own knack would have gone, sprang cautiously after. But the knack had not gone. She chased Emma along the top of the hedge, looking down at the brambles and the early roses, down further at the cow parsley and the banks of grass above the dusty lane. And suddenly a startled bird rose up out of the hedge and skimmed away from them, with startled eye and beat of wing, and left below a nest filled by naked baby birds, gape-beaked for food.

Looking back Charlotte saw the sun-warmed village, the one television aerial belonging to Baby Fumpkins' parents sticking up amid red chimneys. All about, the buttercup meadows were extra patches of sun. The hills rose round behind, a glint of sea showing through them, far away. It was a view Charlotte saw every day from grandfather Elijah's garden, but never before from airy space above a hedge.

So held by it was she that she forgot she did not know how to hover, and had to come heavily to ground in the lane to save herself from landing amid the thorns of the hedge. She was shut-in again, the view was gone, thus common sense came back to her.

'Emma,' she called urgently to her sister, who was still skimming carelessly along the hedge top. 'Emma, come down. Someone might see you there.'

'You are an old fusspot, Char,' Emma said sulkily, and then, 'but I did promise. P'raps we'd better be careful.' So though they flew home, they stayed in the lane itself and were cautious round corners.

But it took so much longer to come up the lane playing as they did that they were late for tea. Even lazy Miss Gozzling was cross with them, mainly because, being lazy, she liked a long rest between tea and supper; she threatened to report them to their grandfather who had spent that day in the town and was not waiting to scold them himself. Miss Gozzling's chest heaved in time with her creaky voice as she scolded, and she tugged at her red and purple beads till they snapped apart and rolled all over the floor. Emma giggled; but Charlotte, seeing a chance of regaining favour, said tactfully, 'Oh, poor Miss Gozzling,' and bent down to pick them up, tugging at Emma's skirt as she did so to make her do the same. By the time they had found every bead, Miss Gozzling had almost forgotten why she was scolding; she gave them some sweet, stale biscuits as a reward and stayed so long talking while they ate their tea that they began to burst with fear there'd be no time for flight before bedtime.

'Emma,' said Charlotte, when at last they were outside, 'Emma, we've got to be careful; grown-ups are going to be a nuisance!'

'I know,' said Emma, serious for once, and sucking her right thumb in the left-hand corner of her mouth, which was a sign that she was thinking.

'They mustn't suspect *anything*,' continued Charlotte. 'They'd only say it was dangerous or something, and we mustn't speak to strange boys.' So they pledged their own pledge to be careful, crossing each other's hearts with fingers dipped in the mossiest of the rain barrels by the far greenhouse.

But caution was hard that night, and nobody came. They explored the garden from the air, and it was new, though they knew it so well. Never before had they seen the tops of the trees in the garden or startled the birds that nested in them. Astonished rooks rose heavily, flapped and cawed and settled back again, cawing softly.

'Well and bless me buttons if they bain't as agile a pair o'little misses as I ever seed,' said old warty Bomble, suddenly catching sight of their faces peering at him from the topmost branches of the tallest copper-beech tree on the wide lawn. 'And wouldn't I 'ave thought as they'd've 'ad to 'ave flown to get to the top of that old fellow!'

# 8

The next morning when they woke up, it was raining. Miss Gozzling made them put on their dark blue mackintoshes, and they set out gloomily for school, scuffing their feet on the wet gravel, their noses filled with the smell of wet earth. No swallows flew on the lawn, and the rain dripped from the trees in the drive onto their heads. On this, the third morning, the boy did not wait for them in the lane. In school he sat motionless beside Maggot Hobbin.

The rain stopped its steady beat halfway through the morning, and a gleam of sun came through tattered clouds and made the raindrops on the windows glimmer and shine. At the sudden brightness Charlotte looked up from her history book to find Maggot and the boy departed. Maggot did not reappear till a quarter past three in the afternoon, when it grew suddenly darker again and started to rain.

After school she came up to Charlotte. 'We're coming to tea with you today,' she said with her usual calmness. 'Is that good?'

'Yes,' replied Charlotte, 'yes,' a little doubtfully now it had come to the point, remembering the strange look of the boy, doubting her grandfather's answer. Maggot, aware, said quickly, 'He will remain unseen—but I haven't his power of invisibility. Should I come?'

'Oh, *yes*,' answered Charlotte immediately, hoping she had not hurt her. 'Oh yes. Grandfather sometimes says we should ask people to tea.' But they never had, because most of the children were frightened of Aviary Hall.

The boy joined them as they came out of the yard. Looking at the sky, it seemed as if the day were almost gone, although it was still only four in the afternoon. It grew steadily darker, not the sudden darkness of thunderstorm but slow-falling darkness of bad weather settling in. The rain, from drizzling, changed to pouring, and from pouring became an endless steady streaming.

The boy and Maggot did not mind the rain. They ran ecstatic, their heads back, drinking it in with open mouths, their eyes shut like worshippers. Maggot's hair fell in wet streamers down her back, and the raindrops coursed on her face, but the boy seemed to have a duck's gift of shaking water from him wholly.

'He's the water bird now,' thought Charlotte, walking miserably with Emma, who had a cat's hatred of wet. Their heads were down; their bare legs brushed against the grass at the side of the lane, dripping grass, which showered cold, wet drops uncomfortably down their legs. Charlotte's misery grew with the likeness she sensed between the two wild creatures, Maggot and the boy, that she herself had not; it was clear especially now as they ran wild in the wet and she crept along the hedge.

But at last there was warmth, dry clothes, and comfort again—teatime. Grandfather Elijah seemed in jovial mood. He sat Maggot down beside him and told her long stories of the days when her great-uncle had been game-keeper, and there had been great shooting parties at Aviary Hall.

'Your great-uncle,' he boomed, 'he was a good feller—only man I ever knew to poach a pair of peacocks to make his wife a bedspread—it was a shame I caught him. But I let him keep his peacocks: nasty noisy birds, peacocks,

34

no loss really. Do you remember your great-uncle, girl?'
he asked Maggot, but her soft voice saying she did and
that the bedspread still was on her own bed could not
penetrate his deafness, and he was off again, teasing them
for their appetites because the food disappeared so
rapidly. That was very true. Miss Gozzling, bringing in a
fresh pot of tea, watched scandalized as two scones
followed each other onto Emma's plate and a moment
later vanished.

'You're greedy, Miss,' she whispered as she passed
Emma's chair, which made Emma giggle and choke.

'That'll make you eat more slowly,' boomed Grandfather Elijah, smiling as Charlotte thumped her back.
The boy—invisible, deliberate, and wicked—removed a
slice of cake from Charlotte's plate this time and ate it,
allowing Miss Gozzling's scandalization to rest on a
demure and innocent Charlotte. Then he removed five
small cakes in rapid succession from a plate at the table
centre. By now Miss Gozzling wasn't capable of scolding
anybody; she scuttled from the room in defeated horror,
and the boy, still invisible, watched, laughing, as she
went. Charlotte feared that soon there would be no secret
any more, that Miss Gozzling would call alarm or their
grandfather notice something strange, but the boy had
finished with food and went, wicked, to lean on the back
of the grandfather's knobbled chair.

Grandfather Elijah was nearly bald but for a strange
lock of hair that clung to his bald dome and was curled
carefully across his brow. When he was vehement, it fell
forward and he flicked it back into place with a crabby
hand. The boy somehow managed to separate a lock of
his own hair and twist it to the same shape, and when the
grandfather talked too hard to Maggot and the lock fell
down, the boy's did the same; likewise, when the lock

was flicked back, the boy did identically that. Maggot remained grave and listening, though there was a smile behind her eyes, but Emma unashamedly giggled, and Charlotte, well-brought-up Charlotte, giggled unashamedly too. Grandfather Elijah, who liked little girls demure, frowned soon and lost his good temper and would be soothed by none, even when Miss Gozzling busied her way back to see what was happening in the dining room. Then grandfather got up and frowned at the dining room and at the innocent Miss Gozzling.

'You disgrace me, grand-daughters,' he said and stamped to his study to read about astrology, which since yesterday had become his great new interest in life, no one knew why.

Charlotte tried to scold the boy, but all he said was, 'Foolish!' and, 'Now I want to see the marble bath,' declaring this as he regarded a pair of elephant's feet stools at the foot of the sombre stairs.

Maggot frowned when she was asked if she would come to see the marble bath too. 'Please,' she replied, 'please, Charlotte, can I not come? I hate the upstairs of houses.'

'Emma can take you somewhere else,' said the boy firmly. Emma almost protested that she too wanted to see the Roman bath, but Maggot was smiling at her, and she felt her too kind to hurt. So she frowned at Charlotte, glared at the boy, and took Maggot away to see the humming-birds.

Meanwhile, Charlotte and the boy climbed the heavy staircase to the bathroom. It had purple and green mosaic fish in the marble of the floor and ceiling. It also had lace curtains at the window, put there by some prudish ancestor, though no one could possibly look in, but these were yellow-stained with age; so was the mottled bath bottom, and the marble steps were chipped and marked. Still it was a bath you stepped down into, and the boy, gravely concentrated, stepped in and out of it several times while Charlotte watched admiringly and thought him wonderful.

'Where does the water come from?' He startled her by asking. She showed him the marble knob set into an alcove in the wall, pulling it out so that warm water sprang from a hole near the bottom of the bath. They watched it fill, heaving mysteriously as the hole was submerged and the water rose, welling from below its own surface. The boy quite suddenly jumped into the middle of it making a gigantic splash. He soaked Charlotte and covered the floor with rivulets of water. Miss Gozzling came at the sound of the splash, but she could not see him mocking in the bath, water running off him, and had to scold Charlotte in a surprised way because she would never have suspected her of such naughtiness.

'Miss Emma now maybe, but not you, Miss Charlotte, and no rhyme or reason that I can see—all alone in the marble bathroom after tea. Come to think, you behaved very badly today, you and Miss Emma, so greedy at table and then giggle, giggle, giggle to annoy your grand-father—and all in front of that nice little girl who talked so nice and ate so dainty, and I was ashamed of you. Get downstairs now to your sister and stay good or I'll tell your grandfather of you, that I will.' But she never would, Charlotte knew. She was too lazy for trouble, and this would create it. So they left her mopping and muttering to herself, and descended the heavy staircase running their hands down the twisted banister.

The boy, dry again, was grinning widely. But he said, 'Thank you, Char,' gratefully, and, 'I'm sorry if there's

37

trouble,' looking anxious for her. Charlotte jumped down the last steps with pleasure at him, and they went into the drawing room to find Emma and Maggot sitting by the humming-birds talking—or rather Emma was talking while Maggot listened.

'You're wet, Charlie,' said Emma in surprise. 'Did he splash you, naughty boy?' but the two of them would say nothing and smiled at each other. So then Emma cried, 'Council of war, we must have a council of war; you said we must have one. What shall we call it—operation flying-school?' she asked, remembering the war books their grandfather Elijah had read before he discovered astrology.

They settled down under the plants by the bow window to discuss the order in which the school children should be taught to fly. Jammy Hat was decidedly the worst at keeping secrets, Molly Scobb nearly as bad. They were to come last of all, and next to them boastful Baby Fumpkins and then Scooter Dimple who talked unceasingly but worshipped Bandy Scragg and if ordered to silence by him would speak only under torture. Immediately before him must come stolid Annie Feather and before her Marly Scragg who could not possibly be kept from any secret concerning her brother for more than one day. Before these two, Bandy, and before him Totty Feather and Ginger Apple; this pair was the great problem. Ginger was a football player, the tough type, and all the school looked up to him and did what he told them; but it thought nothing of little Totty Feather who nipped about busily and wore spectacles. Yet it was Totty Feather that told Ginger what to do, had the cleverest head in the school, and could talk Miss Hallibutt off her teacher's platform. If Totty was told first, Ginger might grow red and sad, and some of the

38

school might think him insulted and make trouble for everyone: but if Ginger was told first, he would be lost without Totty and maybe stupid enough to tell all to Totty, his mate, but without making him realize the importance of silence: he might indeed give him such a sense of hurt pride it would lead to mischief—and Totty had a great gift for mischief; that they all knew. Totty must know first, they decided; he and the boy would have to placate Ginger and the rest of them as they were both capable of doing.

It was growing late. Soon Emma would be called to bed because she was only ten; and although Charlotte, who was twelve, went half an hour later, Maggot would have to depart now and with her the boy. Briefly it had stopped raining though the skies glared. The children went speedily round the garden and into the walled kitchen garden, which was Charlotte and Emma's favourite place, where weeds flourished and fruits were jungle size. The currant bushes were huge and prickly and hung now with raindrops for berries; white flowers bloomed under the wet strawberry nets, which shook water onto the backs of the children as they sought in vain for early fruit.

Out here Charlotte noticed again the kinship between the boy and Maggot, which had strangely disappeared in the house, though she noticed, too, that in spite of this he talked mostly not with herself nor with Maggot, but with Emma. After the adventure of the Roman bathroom, she did not mind especially. But she was sad as they waved goodbye down the gloomy drive, sad because such small funny tea parties could not happen when all the children had learned to fly. And she was also happy; happy as the lone swallow dipping over the lawn, though there was sorrow in the loneness of that.

PART TWO

# 1

Two school weeks it took for them all to learn. The rain went as suddenly as it had come, and they were blazing, golden weeks, split by an enormous storm, which lit and battered half a Sunday night and sent Emma cowering to Charlotte's bed and Charlotte to stand fascinated and awed at the window to watch it. The next morning the sun caught sparkle on every leaf and the air smelled fresh and wet—it was like the beginning of the world morning. Charlotte wished desperately that she could start again, that it was her turn to learn to fly in the glittering buttercup meadow. But it was the turn of Scooter Dimple who was so excited after school that he jumped too high, too obviously into the air and had to be spoken to severely in a corner by Bandy Scragg.

There was a feeling of suppressed excitement in the school, mounting each day as another learned. The children became silent and stood in groups or alone looking at each other sideways with wondering eyes. Could this really happen to others—was it really true? Less and less they played at football and skipping rope in the yard; more and more they put their heads in the sky and watched for birds. Those who did not know, who had not learned, grew worried and lonelier as each day their numbers evaporated like water in the sun. The rest did not fly together yet. It was as if they were waiting for something: waiting in half-shyness for someone else to move. They were self-conscious, like people with songs to sing yet frightened of showing their voice.

But on Thursday Jammy learned. 'I can fly, I can fly! I can fly!!' he squeaked, breathless, after school, hardly out of Miss Hallibutt's hearing. 'So can I!' they all shouted and chattered sparrow-like again, 'Isn't it super? What are we going to do? Where shall we go?'

Charlotte chattered with the rest: she felt that they respected her as the first learner and was proud. But the boy was stern. They had to wait till Saturday to meet and plan together, on the hills above the village. And they must be careful and remember their promise of silence. They all grew solemn and promised again. No one wanted to spoil everything by grown-up discovery, so they went home on their feet not talking but thinking happily of flight.

Never had children hurried so eating their breakfast on Saturday. Parents hardly had time to say, 'George, drink your milk,' or, 'Ginger, come down to breakfast at once!' They were up and fed and out before nine. Charlotte and Emma told Miss Gozzling that they were going to play with Maggot, and their grandfather Elijah said: 'Oh yes, the peacock child,' absent-mindedly stroking his lock of hair before going off to a morning's astrology in his study.

By half past nine they were all on the Downs, gathered on the short tough grass, still wet. There was sharp-smelling thyme and little lady's slipper, yellow and red, clinging close to the earth under the huge sky, where the larks spiralled shrill and high. But no boy came yet.

They waited in their own ways. Totty sat next to Ginger and pointed at the village below. 'That's your house, that's ours, that's the Scraggs'!' and so on. When he had finished that, he talked about something else. He always talked. Ginger said: 'Mmm,' occasionally. Marly and Bandy Scragg had a competition to see which of them could stand for longest on their heads and, having done so, started to fight because Bandy said he had lasted longest and Marly said she had. But it was a friendly fight. They rolled over and over, entangling long arms and legs, and occasionally stopped and lay panting on the grass side by side, grinning identical wicked grins. Scooter Dimple also tried to stand on his head, imitating them, but quite unsuccessfully, and having fallen over several times in a way that would have broken anyone else's neck, began playing with Jammy Hat.

First amiably, they found little spiders and tried to race them on the wiry grass. Then they lay, ears pressed to the ground, because Jammy said they might hear horses coming from miles off; but they heard nothing, though the thyme smelled strong in their nostrils and the rough grass prickled their faces. Meanwhile, Baby Fumpkins sat silently and solidly by himself, his arms clasped round his knees.

Annie and Molly talked domestically in whispers, hair ribbons bobbing. Emma, who had spent less time with these two in the last days, sat where Charlotte and Maggot were beside each other on the grass, wordlessly looking back down to the village, and the trees and the yellow buttercup meadows.

Soon the grass, which had been wet at first, grew drier and more pungent beneath the cloudless sky. The wide silence overcame the chatter. They were half afraid in it that everything had been a dream, that the boy would never come. But no one spoke his fear. They sat there, silently looking.

He came at last. He seemed unconcerned at their waiting, laughed because they were impatient; and they were so glad that he had come that they only said,

'Hullo,' joyfully to him, though Bandy Scragg growled under his breath, 'Late, aren't you?' as his father said to him when he was slow in delivering the meat from the truck on alternate Saturdays.

The boy, hearing, said too politely, 'Am I not wanted?' and Bandy grinned, unperturbed.

'Joke, sir,' he said cheekily. Totty sniggered.

Charlotte, peacemaking, whispered to the boy: 'You must start the meeting. What are you going to say?'

He smiled at her, birdlike. 'What shall I say? I know nothing of meetings.'

Before Charlotte could wonder what to suggest, Totty, who had heard the boy's question, leaned forward confidently and said: 'We gotter form a *Society*, that's what, something proper like they do in London. I could draw up the rules, and we must swear an oath all secret like they do on the television.' (He looked sideways at Baby who had the only television set in the village.) 'Couldn't we have masks?' he pleaded, ideas coming swiftly to his head. But nobody wanted masks: they only wanted to fly.

Yet the oath, they agreed, had to be taken. 'Some of us ain't very good at keeping secrets,' said Bandy, looking meaningly at Jammy Hat, who blushed.

'What sort of oath, then?' asked the boy; and there was silence as they all sat thinking. It must be a very solemn oath.

Charlotte said uncertainly, 'Emma and I . . .' But no one seemed to hear her. The words disappeared in the hot still air. So she pulled her courage further and said, 'Emma and I,' rather more loudly.

'Yes, what?' asked Totty. 'What do you and Emma do?' and suddenly it was she telling them, her voice, hardly believing itself, loud on the Downs.

'Emma and I, we have an oath, a very solemn oath

44

which we swear and we dip our hands in the rain barrels and cross ourselves and promise—would that be solemn enough?' she asked. And they all said yes that was quite solemn enough.

The difficulty was that up here there was no water anywhere in sight. 'Blood, then,' said Bandy ghoulishly.

'Pricked from our arms and all mixed up,' added Marly joyfully, but Molly Scobb looked shrill and said that she wouldn't have anything to do with anything that hurt.

'Yes, nasty goings on that would be,' agreed Annie Feather, ponderous as her mother. Totty glowered at his sister.

'Blood,' said Jammy Hat in a high, squeaky voice, which was clearly meant as an imitation of Molly Scobb; then 'Blood!' gloatingly in a medium voice; then 'Blood!' slowly in a deep, growling voice. Then he burst out laughing and dug Scooter in the ribs, and the two rolled on the ground mock fighting.

'Shut up, you,' said Ginger, warning, and they sat up innocently. The rest looked round at each other. Bandy produced a scout knife and handled it lovingly, watching the others. But none of them except him and perhaps Marly, who pointedly rolled up her sleeve, which was already short, none of them especially wanted to be pricked.

Charlotte, hating blood, tried to screw up her courage but found it hard. Annie and Molly looked as though they would go if the suggestion was carried out. 'I'm not having nothing to do with it,' said Annie firmly, 'not nothing.'

So it was with relief that they heard Totty say, 'Spit, that's what!' It seemed a good idea, solemn enough, something of themselves mingled to enforce their swearing. And though Charlotte privately thought it horrid and the two girls, Annie and Molly, openly turned up their noses, none of them wanted to hold up flying any more, and the others thought it was a wonderful idea, especially the boy who, after being strangely awkward and abruptly spoken at first, was growing in command.

They all spat into a hollow made in the ground; and before the spit could dissolve into the earth, each of them in turn spoke Charlotte and Emma's oath after Charlotte, while the boy dipped his finger in the spit and crossed their hearts for them. 'And may we all die in *agony* if we tell,' they repeated together at the end solemnly. Then they stopped and were silent, looking at the boy.

'Now we're a society,' said Totty. And they were silent again, all of them knowing what they wanted but strangely shy of admitting it.

'And now let's go flying,' Jammy cried, springing to his feet, 'let's go flying,' and so they went, rising in the air behind the boy, the first flight together.

The boy led, Charlotte and Maggot close behind and then the others, air suddenly in them, after the close sun below. They were flying consciously as best they could to show how good at it they were. They flew the whole morning, went home regretfully to lunch, and flew all the afternoon, but through the woods because it was so hot on the Downs in the glaring sun. Here they discovered treetop skimming, looking down through beech and aspen leaves to the wood floor. When they were tired, they lay on the ivied ground by the stream and ate sweets in sleepy silence, staring up at the beech-leaf pattern and the silver glimmer of aspen leaves above them. They were happy—happier even than sparrows because sparrows can always fly. But they were the only flying children.

# 2

On the following Monday morning, something happened that they had been afraid of. Despite their oath, Jammy Hat, too excited by his new skill, forgot that there should be no flying in the schoolyard and bounced into the air just as Miss Hallibutt came out through the big green door. He did not see her come. 'Look at me,' he cried, flying backwards and turning sharply in mid-air. 'I bet no one else can do that 'cept me.'

Miss Hallibutt stared up at him, her mouth open.

'James Hat,' she said loudly in her sternest voice. Jammy started and fell with an uncomfortable bump to the ground. He stood in front of her, his head hanging, very sheepish, and not daring to look at the faces of the others as they gathered round in fearful curiosity, wondering what would happen next.

'James,' she said more gently. 'What were you doing just now?'

'Please, Miss, I was flying,' he whispered, scarlet in the face.

'And how did you learn to do that?' she asked him.

'Please, Miss,' he stammered, 'I . . . I . . . was taught.'

'And who, may I ask, taught you?' Totty, standing behind Miss Hallibutt, made frantic faces at Jammy to say as little as possible and on no account to mention anything about the boy.

'Please, Miss, I . . . I . . . please I was just taught.'

47

The children sighed with relief. The boy was saved for the moment. But although Miss Hallibutt left that point, she had not finished.

'James,' she said very gently. 'I'm sure you're not alone in this. What about the others; can they fly too? Tell me, James.'

Jammy blushed further and hung his head, his mischief gone in his shame before the others at what he had done to impress them. But he would not answer.

Miss Hallibutt lifted her eyes from him and looked round at the watching children.

'You others,' she said. 'Tell me, can you all do this too? Surely James is not by himself.' She looked round the faces, seeking one to question.

'Charlotte?' she said. 'How about you? Can you fly?'

Charlotte, who knew she could not lie convincingly, blushed as red as Jammy. 'Yes,' she said miserably, 'I can fly.'

But Totty and the others had no time to glare at her, for the boy, who had been whispering to Maggot, suddenly stepped forward.

'Don't worry,' he said very quietly to the circle of children. 'I think she's to be trusted.' Then he made himself visible to Miss Hallibutt. 'They can all fly,' he stated dramatically, the red light in his eyes.

'And I taught them,' he added grandly. (Charlotte saw that he was enjoying himself hugely.)

'So you taught them. I am glad to know,' said Miss Hallibutt.

None of them could quite make out the expression on her face. It was not angry, and it certainly was no expression of fear or even puzzlement; she seemed to accept the boy as just another child to be taught and scolded. But it was a very strange expression on her

48

usually correct face. Charlotte, looking at her, half wondered if it were not almost an expression of envy.

There was silence in the yard: a bird sounded from the meadow; a pigeon purred softly in a chestnut tree. The sun beat on their bare heads. They all watched the boy and their schoolteacher in their midst and waited for her to speak.

Then Miss Hallibutt, grim Miss Hallibutt, playing agitatedly with her spectacles cord, said breathlessly:

'I suppose . . . I suppose . . . I cannot learn to fly too?'

In their astonishment they looked at the boy, looked from him back to Miss Hallibutt, from her back to him again.

The boy said apologetically: 'No, I can only teach children—you are too old.'

'Yes, I feared that,' said Miss Hallibutt sadly. 'You are lucky children. I always wanted to fly at your age—once. And I suppose as you're here,' she said to the boy, 'I suppose you had better come to school. And mind you behave.

'But gracious me, children,' she cried suddenly, looking at her watch. 'It's well after nine o'clock. I must fetch the bell or there will be no work done this morning.' And she flustered back into the school, her hair falling down.

The children left behind looked after her, feeling strangely disturbed and sad despite the sunlight. They felt sorry for her but also sad for themselves because they had suddenly realized, for perhaps the first time, that they too would have to grow up and that this golden flying summer could not go on forever. Marly, rarely serious, said gravely:

'I suppose we won't be able to fly either for long.'

They were all thinking the same except perhaps

49

Jammy, and they knew she was right. So they went in more silently than usual at the summons of the big brass bell.

After that, the boy came visibly to their lessons. He was not spared the lash of Miss Hallibutt's tongue, and it seemed that sometimes he regretted his visibility. The children could never quite understand how it was that she asked him no questions about himself as most grown-ups would be bound to, insistent on an answer—as they in fact in their curiosity wanted to themselves. But she never appeared to show even faint interest in his mystery. They wondered if perhaps it was because she had known someone like him when she was a child. Whatever the truth, she seemed to them now a little as they themselves were, a person, not just someone who taught them arithmetic and geography and spelling.

# 3

Miss Hallibutt's discovery of their secret was really the saving of it, for Jammy Hat out of shame became the best keeper of the secret from parents instead of the worst. It made all of them more careful, but him it turned into a clam. It also meant that school hours, when they were gathered together in the sight of a grown-up, were not the continual difficulty they might have been had they still considered Miss Hallibutt an enemy, liable as parents to disapprove. On the other hand, under her watchful eye they could not spend the remaining months of the school term skipping homework to go flying or trying some of the wilder expeditions they had planned. These would have to wait until the term had ended and Miss Hallibutt had returned to her home in the suburbs. Thus, most of the rest of June and nearly the whole of July they spent learning to fly better, finding out how to do things like flying backwards or turning swiftly in mid-air and in discovering their own special skill in flight or lack of it.

They all flew very differently, some much more skilful than others. The boy and Maggot alone were wholly birdlike, jointless creatures of the air; the boy eagle-like, Maggot more graceful, a swift perhaps or a martin. Of the others, Marly and Bandy were best, in a gymnastic way. They were easy and fearless but somehow angular, lazy as rooks, without the grace of swallows. Totty Feather darted eager as a wagtail, and Ginger Apple was no bird at all, his flight all bulk and hard work like his football;

but he was strong enough to last longer than most and to look more dangerous in the air. Annie Feather flew slowly, heavily, dully, yet she was sound: much sounder than Molly Scobb who tried to imitate Maggot Hobbin but quite without success, continually entangling herself in branches and losing her hair ribbon or landing herself in gorse bushes and bursting into tears. Emma Makepeace was much more stoical; she flew fast and fearless but choppily, so that she quickly tired, and her landings were not graceful. Scooter Dimple, who tried to be as fearless as his hero Bandy, was apt as Molly Scobb to get into tangles, though he remained cheerful. Worst of all fliers was Baby Fumpkins. He could only fly short distances without having to rest and when teased about it was inclined to sulk. The others called him Jemima Puddle-Duck because that was how he flew.

As for Jammy Hat, being so young and so small, flying came as naturally to him as walking. He flew just as he walked and swam, sticking his bottom out, wriggling between people, trying tricks and turns all the time, which dropped him on the ground.

It was Jammy who had the idea of using frog flippers in the air. 'You can swim faster with 'em, why not fly?' he shouted suddenly, and he was right and clever—there was a kick and push in the frog-feet, which sent all of them skimming more swiftly through the air, with the speed of champions. Even the boy was better with them. Kicking his feet fiercely, he could move long distances, motionless as a diver, but curving upward to heat of sky, not downward to cool water; and they made Charlotte feel that she too was flying, not struggling wearily, as so often it seemed when skill was gone. In reality, she was not a bad flier: she flew cautiously yet with an elegance that she did not know she possessed. The boy said to her

52

one day, 'You look nice flying, Charlotte,' which made her blush with pleasure and start to say thank you, only to find that he had gone again, darting far on ahead with Maggot Hobbin.

It was the third Saturday in July that day and a great day for them, for it was their first expedition together flying, the one expedition they made while it was still termtime. It had been a scalding week, so hot that the classroom, all its windows open, cooked tempers slowly to simmering. On Friday afternoon, Miss Hallibutt had surveyed the school searchingly through her spectacles before dismissing them on the dot of four o'clock as usual. But she had not given them any homework; and she beckoned the boy back with an authoritative finger. Had she forgotten their work, the children wondered as they gathered their books together, hastening to escape in case it was only a mistake. They scuttled from the classroom into the schoolyard before she might remember, though not without curious glances at the boy smiling a smile that was wild and beaky as Miss Hallibutt talked into his listening ear. In a moment he followed them into the yard and, still smiling, beckoned them through the high iron gates into the meadow on the other side of the railings where the chestnuts stood.

'She says we're to go tomorrow—somewhere cool,' he had said, 'and not to overexert ourselves or alarm your parents. We can go!' he sang out gladly, lively as sunlight with pleasure. 'Where shall we go, I, you, all of us?' So they reflected and decided with little argument to go to the lake, their favourite place, where sometimes they went to play.

It stood in a parkland that once had surrounded a house long vanished but for a few scattered bricks and cracked concrete flooring. The lake itself, a little way away, was wild and overgrown, birdful and rush-fringed. There was a small temple overlooking its water and the children loved it, though it was too far away to visit often, and they usually only went in the school holidays when they could spend a whole day there at a time. Flying, they would arrive more quickly, and so they planned their day, tempers forgotten in the thought of freedom.

Charlotte pretended confidence, but she desperately feared that they should not be allowed a whole day from home. It was not a thing they had ever asked before. Emma said grandly that she would go anyway, whatever anyone said, but Charlotte was frightened that if this happened, their chance of flying with the others would be spoiled for the whole summer. However, she said nothing to anyone, and when she tentatively asked Miss Gozzling in her most tactful voice if they might go, she was surprised by the enthusiasm with which Miss Gozzling said, 'Of course, dears, if your grandpa allows it,' for Miss Gozzling, idle, saw a lazy day ahead. As for Grandfather Elijah himself, he was absent-minded these days, reading astrology in his study. He shouted at Emma's manners at teatime, but he only said again, 'Will that peacock child be there?' and on hearing that she would, said, 'Of course, grand-daughters. Shall Miss Gozzling give you luncheon?' and retired as usual to his study.

The others too had found permission easy. Baby Fumpkins, to all their surprise, had defied his anxious mother to come, though in his defiance he blushed red at regular intervals all day and said doubtfully, 'What will Mother say?' Jammy and Scooter told their mothers that they would spend the day at each other's houses, which, living at opposite ends of the village, was not likely to be discovered. The rest of them were old enough or came from large enough families to make their mothers glad of a day's peace, asking no dangerous questions.

So they gathered early on the Downs, some with, some without picnics, and flew to the lake over fields and a small wood, and from thence to smooth parkland, where a delicate-stepping deer herd snuffed into air below them, soft eyes wide, too surprised at humans who flew over their heads to disappear, smoothly leaping into the distance, or to melt their dappled shadows into the trees, as they usually did, when disturbed. The boy called out to them and they relaxed, their sloe eyes curious as they watched the school fly by.

And suddenly below them was the lake. In excitement Jammy forgot to hold himself in flight and plummeted out of the air, to land splash in the water, his round face opened wide in surprise, eyes, mouth gaping. 'It's lovely,' he said, as he came up spluttering, not minding their laughter. 'It's smashing, honest. Let's all swim. Bet I can swim faster than you.' And he grabbed at Scooter's dangling leg and pulled him down into the water too, shouting with laughter. The rest of them said 'Babies,' in a superior way, and landed sedately on the bank. But the sun was very hot, and the water looked cool in the rushless pool in the centre. They had all brought bathing suits with them, so except for Molly and Baby who could not swim, they threw off their clothes and fell into the lake impatiently.

Sadly, it turned out more muddy than deep. The mud rose in squirls round their toes, and ducks and moor hens scattered, frightened, into the weeds.

Charlotte swam very well, and she loved ducks and had watched them often on the village pond, diving for bread or skimming down onto the water from the air. So it was she who tried tentatively to duck-land, flying high from the bank and landing, legs outstretched and feet tight together, slanting upwards like skis or the flippers of a flying boat. The first time she tried, she landed unevenly and fell sideways into the water, swallowing a mouthful of it. It tasted horribly of mud and weeds, and some went up her nose, to make her splutter and cough. The next time, the same thing happened; indeed, she fell harder, flat onto the water, and stung her face scarlet. She almost gave up trying, but suddenly she noticed the boy watching her and tried again, desperately, refusing to fail before his mocking eyes. And this time it worked.

She landed straight, in a rush of water like a duck, and slid to a sitting position. She looked triumphantly at the boy to prove herself. She did not speak to him yet; she went back to the land and tried the same thing again: and again it worked. 'Look at me,' she cried out in pride, forgetting her reserve. 'This is super,' and she did it again while they all watched. They were very impressed, and she was proud; but the boy was laughing at her. She was suddenly embarrassed at her display and blushed bright pink.

'Why are you doing that?' the boy asked teasingly, snatching at an insect.

'Does it seem a bit boasting?' she asked doubtfully, feeling the red mount in her face.

'And why not?' he asked, eating the insect with enjoyment. 'None of them thought of it. It was really quite clever of you,' he added, darting off like a dragonfly to the other side of the lake.

# 4

Charlotte felt tired; she was glad to lie on the bank by herself while the others practised duck landings noisily on the water. It was a beautiful lake, she decided. She would like to live there for ever and ever: and lying there now, there seemed no reason why she should ever move.

The lake was not big. On the side where Charlotte was lying the parkland stretched down to it: a scattering of tall, smooth beech trees and lengths of sheep-cropped grass. On the other side of the lake, the woods began. Vast rhododendrons, overgrown, reached almost to the edge of the water and threw their long sober leaves into it. In a clearing, fighting for life among the bushes, was the small temple, a round dome on slender pillars planted on a round marble floor. Shallow steps now broken and overgrown stretched down to the reeds and the water, and carved above the archway overlooking these was the head of a goddess: at least Charlotte was sure she must have been a goddess once. She was very pagan; but her nose was broken, and ivy curled rakishly over her brow.

'That's Old Moo,' said Totty informatively to Emma when they all sat down to eat their lunch.

Charlotte said, 'Oh!' in surprise. 'Why?' she asked.

Once, Totty told her with delight, a cow had found its way into the bushes behind the temple and had stuck there, plaintively bellowing. 'That's a ghost,' Totty had said decisively. 'Oooh,' the others who were with him had cried, allowing themselves to be frightened. 'Yus.

57

The ghost of the lady over the door,' Totty had gone on, his imagination leaping. 'Oooh,' the rest had said again, though they knew it must be a cow. Ever since then the goddess of the temple had been known as Old Moo.

The boy eating one of Charlotte's spam sandwiches (she hated spam) was not impressed. He was cross anyway because it was early to be eating and he wanted to explore; but the others, especially Ginger, said their insides were flapping, just flapping, and they didn't care if it was still only eleven o'clock in the morning—and it wasn't; it was half past eleven—and they were going to eat. So they did, sprawled on the sheep-cut turf on the other side of the lake from the temple.

Totty and Ginger were delighted to have had their own way. It was more than being glad to eat; they were glad to have won the argument with the boy, whose command Totty, at least, was beginning to resent. Totty's obvious gloating annoyed the boy. He sat by himself, snatching at insects, and took with bare thanks the sandwich that Charlotte offered him. She wondered what she could say to calm him, but looking at how hunched and ruffled he was, like an angry bird, she decided to leave him alone. Indeed, he soon began to recover of his own accord. At first the children were wary of what they said to him, in case he took their power to fly away from them. But soon they forgot their fear, because he forgot his rage and joined their conversation, if not with words, at least with his interest.

When they were full and were beginning to grow restless, Ginger and Totty found some flat stones and started skimming them across the water, competing to see who could make them hop most on the surface. Totty who was very clever at it, better than Ginger despite his smaller strength, managed to make one stone hop seven times, spreading round ripples on the still water.

'Bet you can't do that,' he said to Ginger in a superior voice. Ginger tried and failed, but good-naturedly only laughed, his face pink with trying.

'Told you you couldn't,' remarked Totty, grinning proudly. The boy, who had been watching him with hostility, now wandered over and, picking up a stone, flung it carelessly across the water. All the children watched it, suddenly silent, and counted to themselves . . . one, two . . . six, seven, eight . . . ten, eleven . . . thirteen . . . no fourteen whole times the little stone skimmered on top of the water with light ripple before sinking silently beneath the surface on the fifteenth hop.

The boy snatched at a fly and sauntered away without looking at Totty's scowling. 'Show-off, stuck-up, bet he cheated, bet he used *magic*,' muttered Totty under his breath. 'C'mon, Ginger, let's leave these babies and that cheat,' and they too walked away, purposefully stalking, head high, round the edge of the lake until, faced with an impenetrable thicket of rhododendrons and brambles, they were forced back and foolishly returned.

The ill feeling aroused by this incident did not seem to last. Totty, who was rarely vindictive for long, quickly recovered his temper, while Ginger, who had never been angry anyway, had all cares rubbed from his mind by the sudden friendliness Emma was showing him. As for the boy, he made no further effort to annoy them and with the others was particularly friendly and talkative.

Thus, if they thought of it at all, most of them imagined it only a temporary quarrel, swiftly ended. But Charlotte, although she said to Maggot when they were talking together, 'Oh, I'm sure it's all right now,' Charlotte feared trouble one day; and looking at Maggot, she thought she feared it too. 'It mustn't spoil the summer,' she cried inside herself. 'It mustn't, it mustn't!'

The rest of the day passed swiftly. They swam again and became hungry, in vain because they had no more food. Jammy and Scooter managed to annoy a swan into chasing them, its wings stretched wide and high, dark hissings coming from its beak, poked out angry and orange at the end of a serpentine neck. The boy was forced to fly to their rescue. He talked to the swan in some soundless language that seemed to satisfy it, for it bowed its head and folded its foamy body onto the water and swam away majestically, without a glance at the two frightened boys.

Shortly after this, when the shadow of the temple stretched long on the water, they flew home again. The midges bit savagely, and there was mud dried on their bodies, which were stretched and burned and exercised. They could hardly struggle along and went slower and slower towards home. But, sun- and air-full, they were happy, and their mothers wondered at their appetites.

All that is but Jammy and Scooter's mothers who were too busy scolding them for spending a whole day away and telling lies, for they had met out shopping and discovered the deception. Jammy and Scooter, shut up in their bedrooms without supper, wondered gloomily how they would ever escape again. Baby's mother, on the other hand, was so thankful to see Baby again that she did not scold him and gave him extra ice-cream for supper. It was not fair, said Jammy and Scooter when they discovered this at school on Monday morning. It was not fair. Parents, it seemed, were going to be a problem—so were Totty and the boy, thought Charlotte. And the summer holidays had not even begun.

# 5

Slowly the summer term crept to its end. Usually the children enjoyed the last weeks of school when work became less and play more. But this year, with so much of the air still unexplored (for Miss Hallibutt had only relented on one weekend), the usual pleasures were dull and seemingly endless. Sports day came and went, but how could they enjoy running and jumping in competition with the school from the next village when in the air they could go so much higher, so much faster, and so much freer?

Miss Hallibutt said in school on the Monday after that it was disgraceful, that never in history had they been so badly defeated by the other school; it was unsporting to be so scornful of others' games just because they were lucky enough to be able to fly, and it was only luck that they could. She was ashamed of them all, yes ashamed, especially after she had allowed a weekend without homework so that they might fly; never, she said, never would she be so lenient again.

The children heard her, resentful and barely ashamed, wishing only the tedium of term to end. But the boy apologized with a most charming smile that Charlotte could not believe was real, though looking at him again, she wondered if that was a misjudgement; for the boy liked Miss Hallibutt, and though she was often stern with him, Miss Hallibutt liked the boy. She now became confused at his smile, murmured words about disgraceful, but she supposed understandable, and scolded the school no more. Then the boy smiled at her again, a genuine smile, unmocking and wide, and went back lithely to his place.

Two days later, term ended completely. Miss Hallibutt made each child recite a poetry piece in turn and afterwards said goodbye sternly but almost tearfully. Then she went back to her home in the suburbs. Two months of summer stretched before them.

The complications seemed to have gone. There had been no further rivalry between the boy and Totty since the day by the lake. And the suspicions of parents, it appeared, had been confined to those of Scooter Dimple and Jammy Hat, who had put down their sons' sin to the usual causes, that is, the general tendency to wickedness of Jammy and Scooter, and not to any strange and dangerous activity in which the whole village school took part. So on that warm, almost August day when term ended, there seemed nothing but gloriousness ahead.

But the very next day it started to rain, and it rained without stop for over a fortnight. When it was not raining, the sky frowned and water dripped sadly from everything. It seemed as if the world were dyed a grey which would never wash out.

At first it did not matter very much. The sun had shone for so long that the children welcomed a feel of rain on their faces and the soft running of water everywhere. It was a dissolved and misty world, strange after the hard glitter of sun they had known for so long. They found it good for flying if they ignored how wet their clothes became and how their hair fell damply across their faces or dripped down their necks according to where the wind blew. When the weather was calm and the rain fell straight as a curtain, it was like swimming under water without the effort, wet where skin was bare, on faces, hands, and legs. It was better still when the wind roared and the rain roared too and they battled heroically with the elements of water and air, which beat back each effort of flight they made, till their hair, their eyes, their bodies were filled with them and only their thinking was separate.

But the days when it blew were not frequent. Mostly the rain came down in straight lines. Flying in it even in the first days was only fun for a short time. Then they would become aware that they were wet and draggled and uncomfortable, and huddle like wet birds under the trees, longing miserably for dryness—though when they were dry, they would go quite joyfully out to get wet again, thinking only of the pleasures of rain flight, forgetting the misery. After a few days of this they came down with such streaming colds that their parents clucked and murmured and made them stay indoors while the rain streamed at the windows. They sat, most of them, wretchedly sneezing, in their separate houses and longed for the golden days of termtime when the sun had shone without end.

The boy came round to visit them, banging at their windows and saying crossly that they were all softies (a word he had picked up from Ginger) and it was stupid to give up like this and scatter the flying school just because of rain. None of them, their feet in mustard baths, their chests covered in plasters or their throats choked with camomile or black-currant tea according to their mothers' favourite cures, none of them were very sympathetic towards the boy for scolding them. Even Charlotte said crossly: 'Go away; I don't want to; how can we?' when he begged her come out with him into the rain-soaked garden.

She and Emma sat sneezing alternately in the small dark tower room of Aviary Hall, dabbing at their paint-boxes or looking at books and being cross with one another. Every now and then Miss Gozzling came in to give them large spoonfuls of her own patent cold-cure, which was excessively nasty, and to scold them for their ill temper. But Grandfather Elijah never came because he said that colds were bad for astrology.

When all the colds were gone, the rain still fell. Most days the children gathered together somewhere, in a barn or in the school, which was used as a village hall in holiday time, or, on one day, in Aviary Hall, which had a top storey where nobody ever went. Grandfather Elijah had been surprisingly willing when Charlotte and Emma asked tentatively if their friends might play there. 'As long as they make no noise,' he had said benignly over his soup, 'of course they may, my dears: astrology welcomes the young!' But Totty had the idea of roller skating up there in the long empty passage, and the railway noise that had echoed through the house as a result made Grandfather appear shouting astrological curses and caused the banishment of the school from the house forever or for as long as the grandfather remembered. Charlotte and Emma were kept in for the whole of the next day and were only allowed to join the others on the day after that because the grandfather had discovered some important astrological fact in an ancient book and was too excited to do more than mutter 'Of course, of course,' when Charlotte asked politely for permission.

All that really resulted from the fortnight's rain were quarrels: between Jammy and Scooter, between Emma and Charlotte, between Bandy and Marly, and between Totty and Ginger. They were silly quarrels about nothing and only mattered briefly because they could not fly outside and ideas for indoor games were scarce. But one quarrel was more than just that. The fortnight of rain set fire to the quarrel that had first sprung, on the lake day, between Totty and the boy. Neither ever said much to the other. But the sense of conflict was there all the time, inflamed by the closeness of their lives, while the rain fell steadily.

# 6

One night when the rain had been coming down for nearly two and a half weeks, Charlotte suddenly woke from an unremembered dream. She was not sure that the waking was not itself a dream, as she peered sleepy-eyed through black shadow and silver moonlight, which seemed no more real than the blurring swiftness of the dream. It took her several minutes to realize that there was a full moon staring coldly from a sky without cover.

She leapt out of bed onto the cold linoleum and went to the window to look at it. Only then did she see it was not by chance and moonlight that she had wakened. Something—no, someone—was banging at the windowpane. She shrank back, seeing there a white oval shape—was it a ghost, was it a burglar? Miss Gozzling had told terrible tales of both. Charlotte shivered desperately, wondering where the poker was, for that was always Miss Gozzling's weapon against any intruder, or so she said.

Then a voice called softly, 'Don't be silly, Char! it's only me!' And the white shape took sudden form and face and she saw that it was the boy, and behind him, another shape appeared in the moonlight—Maggot. Charlotte rushed to open the window wider to let them in. When Emma, who had remained fast asleep, woke up, it was to see the three of them conferring under the window conspiratorially.

'Whoever's that?' she cried, afraid, thinking she was still dreaming. 'Only us,' they said. 'Look at the lovely night—we're going out now, all of us. It's much too good to waste asleep, after so much rain.'

But Emma, who read school stories, said, 'We must have a picnic, a proper midnight feast!'

'That's an idea,' they said, so they crept in single line down the stairs to find provisions.

There was little in the larder at the bottom of the stone basement stairs. Miss Gozzling was too lazy to be a storer of pies or bottled fruits or to need many ingredients for cooking. But there was a row of bright-labelled cans on the white shelves lining the walls. Emma said, 'Let's have baked beans; they're lovely cold,' so they took one of these (and a can opener—luckily). Then they found an open box of sugar lumps, and some apples and tomatoes in a basket. Finally they seized an enormous box of chocolate biscuits. 'They must be Miss Gozzling's,' said Emma, giggling. 'She never gives any to us. We'd better call her Miss Guzzling!' and these they removed without conscience or care, though before they had tried not to make their taking too obvious. But Charlotte had a faint twinge of shame about Miss Gozzling, thinking how kind she could be and how terrible to have so many chins.

At last, clasping their loot, they were out in the moonlight. The sisters had leaped from their bedroom above ivied walls, pretending they were fearless as Maggot or the boy. But they were not. Charlotte poised, had a moment of terror, and knew that Emma too was afraid of this open leap into the night. But now it was over, they flew joyously towards the village.

Their horizon was sky, the evening star, cold and white, alone in it but for moonlight, and below the blackness of sky, the deeper black that was the Downs, and on them more stars but human yellow ones. They dropped down to the village, down to the trees, until the horizon was more black hill than moon-black sky. They went round the village in the moonlight and their four faces at the windows woke all the children except Baby Fumpkins, who slept too soundly. Out they came, sleepy-eyed, hair on end, day clothes pulled on over night clothes, to see the glad cold moonlight where rain had been before. 'Cor,' they said or were silent according to their kind. Jammy and Scooter shadow-chased. 'Didn't know the moon gave you shadows too,' they said and chased them up and down in the air and on the ground, shouting at the freedom of it after the weary days indoors.

They flew together into the black woods, where the moonlight came, if at all, in strips and angles, and the dark was very dark; and thence out onto the Downs, the full moonlit Downs, where the gorse flowers were silver instead of yellow, and the thyme close to the earth as cold and grey looked its hard iron tang of a taste.

They were glad of Emma's beans now, of the tomatoes, the apples, and the chocolate biscuits. They ate the beans from the tin, which was difficult without spoons. They had to scoop them out with their fingers, each child in turn, and afterwards wipe their hands clean on the cold turf. Then they gorged on fruit and sugar lumps and chocolate biscuits.

Charlotte, the rough sweet grit of a sugar lump against her tongue, said aloud, 'It must be summer now!'

'Yes,' they all agreed, suddenly grave, 'it must be summer now.'

'Or else it will be school again soon,' she went on. 'September, chestnuts, frost—not flying weather.' They didn't like to think what could happen then, and the boys, in fear perhaps, went mad, as if moonlight had the same effect on them as March is supposed to have on hares.

'Bet you can't do this or that or the other,' they
wagered each other proudly, and became wilder and
wilder in their boasts. Suddenly they were drawing up
sides for some sport or other, boys against boys. 'Jammy,
you come here with me,' said the boy to the smallest
member of the school.

Simultaneously, Totty cried loudly, 'Jammy's with
me; c'me here, Jammy.'

The little boy wavered between them. He turned to the
boy, then to Totty. Next he looked beseechingly at
Charlotte, but she could only give him, in pity, another
lump of sugar. He put his stubby hands to his stubby hair
and rubbed it on end. 'Who called me?' he asked,
hopeful that someone else would decide for him.

'Me,' said Totty and the boy together. Jammy glanced
from one to the other. He made his decision. Sticking his
chin into the air, he marched deliberately over and took
his place beside the boy. 'I'm for 'ere,' he announced
gravely.

'Jammy,' said Totty slowly. 'I chose you, not him; are
you coming?'

'But I,' said the boy stepping between Totty and
Jammy, 'I chose him for myself. He's mine, not yours.'

'Who says?' asked Totty, spectacled and truculent.

'I do,' said the boy.

'Who's you?'

'Me,' said the boy calmly, glinting.

'I said who's you?' said Totty dangerously.

'I, if you'd rather,' came the boy's reply.

Totty exploded. 'Who's you I said—and you won't
say—you can't say, that's what I think, SEE? You're just
an upstart, you are. Where do you come from? What you
doing here? That's what I want to know. I don't believe
you come from anywhere,' he shouted fiercely into the

boy's face, 'anywhere, anywhere, anywhere!' and he threw himself onto the boy, which was brave because he was much smaller and not a good fighter as Ginger was.

They were rolling over on the moonlit grass, the boy all claw like a furious bird holding no strength back. Charlotte thought she should throw herself down to stop them, but thinking of it and watching them lash about, she was not brave enough. The children stood in a still circle watching, alarmed but excited. There was pride in Jammy's stiffened back now that his part was finished. Never in his life before had he been the cause of a fight. And such a good fight at that, for Totty was inspired. But Maggot stepped forward and surveyed them scornfully.

'Stop that,' she said, her voice low. It seemed unlikely in that frenzy they could have heard such an order, yet there was maybe a small lull in the fighting, a very slight hesitation.

'Stop that,' she said again, a little louder; and this time the movement almost ceased. 'You two, stop it,' said Maggot a third time, her voice lower again; and at last the arms and legs stopped flailing altogether and the two faces surfaced among them, Totty's flushed and spectacleless, a black eye appearing, the boy unmarked, though the shell freckles stood out on his cheeks like the hackles of a dog.

'What was that for?' said Maggot shortly. 'Silly idiots. What's the point of fighting on a night like this?'

But none of Totty's wrath seemed abated by the struggle. 'It's him,' he said with a jerk of his head at the boy, as he had seen his father jerk his head at the people he disliked.

'And what of him?' asked Maggot, and all the children waited for an answer.

'He came here,' said Totty. 'He bosses us all—me, Ginger, like all the girls!'

'That's our fault if we let him boss us, not his,' cried Charlotte hotly, forgetting to be shy in the boy's defence. Totty looked at her witheringly.

'Huh, you're soft on him. That's not what I mean anyway. Who is he? We don't know; he don't say; we don't ask. And what's his magic?' he went on, hushed. 'It might be bad magic for all we know, witch sort of magic,' and he paused to let them imagine cauldrons and evil spells. They looked at the boy awed. Surely he couldn't be someone of this sort, the friendly boy who had taught them to fly. Yet he was very strange; and they knew nothing of his beginnings.

'I say he should tell us,' went on Totty, seeing the effect his words had had on them, especially in this cold moonlight on the open Downs. 'Tell us what he is and then he can boss us if it's something good. What do you say, all of you?' he finished, looking round at them standing in a circle.

Ginger, no longer pretending leadership now that leadership had to be explained, stood behind him, half nodding his red head but with some doubt, which was unusual in this unquestioning friend of Totty's. The others looked at one another wondering if Totty might be right. But they wanted mainly to fly; they did not want difficulties such as this one. Jammy and Scooter alone were careless, turning somersaults on the grass.

# 7

Charlotte was sharply aware that this quarrel was not one easily settled. Somehow, something must be decided, otherwise the whole summer would be spoiled; and they would have to think quickly. Totty and the boy were glaring at each other; any minute they would be rolling over and over again on the grass. Maggot had fallen silent. So Charlotte spoke quickly before the fight could start; and the others, who were used by now to Charlotte having good ideas, listened to her eagerly, even Jammy and Scooter, who had stopped turning somersaults.

'Look, there's a fight and it's a proper one, but we mustn't have fights,' she pleaded. 'I read in a book just the other day that in the olden days when kings or lords had wars, they settled them by single fights—duels that is—instead of whole armies fighting.'

'But it's only Totty and the boy fighting anyway,' Emma butted in, trying to keep up with her sister. But Charlotte still had ideas. She paused, puzzled for a second, but was away again fast.

'But you see, it is sort of the same because we don't want them to fight and hurt each other and nor did the kings want their armies to fight and hurt each other. So we could have it the other way round, all of us divided to fight the single battle like an olden-day tournament, though we won't have horses or armour and things.'

'Will we fight proper?' said Annie.

'I won't,' said Molly.

72

'Nor I,' said Annie.

But Bandy and Marly cried out, 'I will,' together, wicked eyes gleaming.

'*No!*' cried Charlotte. '*No*—you haven't heard. Listen to me, all of you,' for they were talking among themselves and they stopped and listened to her again almost respectfully.

'Charlotte, you've got good ideas,' Bandy declared; Charlotte blushed scarlet.

'Look,' she hurried on. 'No, we're not to fight. It'd spoil things. That's why we're fighting so no one'll be hurt, not Totty or the boy. It must be a formal fight like a tournament—you know I read too that they blunted their lances so they wouldn't hurt each other; they only had to get a certain number of hits or something.'

'Yes, that's right,' said Bandy, who knew a little bit about tournaments, because although he wasn't much interested in school, he was interested in battles (which pleased his father, who thought bloodthirstiness a good tendency in a future butcher).

Charlotte nodded at Bandy and went on. 'Well, see, we can't do that, but couldn't we play something and settle the quarrel, something like French and English or kick the can—no, French and English would be better because it's got sides—and then whichever side wins, Totty's or the boy's, he wins the quarrel.'

'But it's *my* quarrel,' cried Totty aggressively, 'nobody else's—except his.' The boy, however, said nothing. All the time since Charlotte had begun to talk, he had been remote, standing apart from the others, looking out from the hill down to where the village lay half visible in the moonlight. Now he had even sat down and appeared to be counting the toes on his feet. But he looked up at Charlotte at this, a fierce look but she thought approving.

So she took courage; more than courage, anger even. She burst out furiously at Totty.

'It's not just your quarrel. You're jealous; you like bossing—that's what it is. And you're going to spoil the whole summer for everybody. NO, if anyone fights, we all will. It belongs to all of us, don't you see?' and she stamped her foot, which gave her great pleasure. In their house it was usually only Emma who stamped her foot. And it seemed to impress the rest of them as they stood there watching her. Totty said no more. Charlotte overcome by her unusual flow of words fell silent.

'But what'll we decide by this fight?' said Bandy. He did not know; Charlotte did not know either. What were they to decide? The rest were looking at her as if she should know—and she did not. She looked at Totty, but he was expressionless. 'What are we to decide like this?' insisted Marly; and there was silence still. Then a voice came out of the darkness; it was the boy's voice, deeper than usual, very fierce, an eagle's voice, if eagles spoke.

'This,' it declared, 'this will be the decision. If I lose, I shall go away; Totty shall lead you. No—don't worry'— for there were anxious questionings springing up— 'don't worry—you shall fly, all of you till the summer is ended. I shan't take that power away.'

'But you must tell us who you are as well,' insisted Totty's voice.

'Yes and that as well,' agreed the boy fiercely. Then there was quiet again. The children stood curiously. It was Jammy who uttered shrilly the question they all asked in their silence.

'And what if you win? What will you win then?'

'The right to stay. Nothing else,' answered the boy calmly.

74

'For how long?' asked Charlotte trying to hide the great fear she had of his going.

'Till the end of the summer,' he answered her, and it was her alone he was answering. 'I can stay no longer . . . but maybe . . . maybe . . .' He left more words unspoken, and she did not ask for them. The maybe were perhaps better ignored for the moment. In any case Jammy Hat was butting in eagerly again.

'Will you tell us about you?' he demanded. 'We couldn't not know ever—I'd die of curiosity,' he added in a grown-up voice, using one of his mother's expressions.

The boy laughed, a mocking laugh that they could hear but hardly see.

'Would you now—how sad!' He was serious suddenly.

'Yes, I will tell you—that I promise,' and they had to be satisfied with that, for he spoke little more as the children chose their sides for the tournament that had to follow from this night's work.

At first it seemed as if the sides would be very uneven. Charlotte, Emma, and Maggot, the three of them joined the boy unhesitatingly. Jammy, who hated both Totty, who 'bossed' he said, and Annie, Totty's sister, who 'bossed still more', joined them also. But the others moved in a block behind Totty: Bandy because Totty was his mate and because he too was somewhat suspicious of the boy. Marly went with her brother because she always did. Scooter, too, though hating separation from Jammy, followed his hero Bandy. Annie joined Totty, partly because he was her brother, even if they did quarrel, partly because she disliked the stuck-upness of Charlotte and Maggot. Molly inevitably followed Annie. That left Baby, who was not with them but snug asleep in bed, and who, it was near certain, would follow the crowd to Totty; it also left Ginger. Nobody bothered to wonder where he would go; he was Totty's mate, Totty's friend; where Totty went, Ginger went too. And that left the boy with three girls and the one smallest boy on his side, or it would have done. But Ginger, redheaded and freckled, red rising under his freckles, though in the moonlight that was hard to see, Ginger hesitated. He started to walk straight over to Totty unthinkingly. But then he looked back and saw Emma. He stood between the sides, turning left and right, confusedly.

'Hurry up, Ging,' said Totty in his most bossy voice, spectacles moonlit, glinting. This was a mistake. Ginger dimly resented an order from his former fellow leader who had now taken full command. To add to his confusion, Emma sang out:

'Come on, Ginger, don't listen to him. Come with us.' To hear his love so encouraging him was almost too much for Ginger, blushing in the moonlight. But still he hesitated, loyal to the boys and Totty.

'Coming,' he said to Totty, but looking back at Emma. At this, Emma, very sweetly, very deliberately, smiled at him, which wholly overcame Ginger. Solid, strong, and acting without Totty for almost the first time in his life, he joined the boy standing opposite Totty, flanked by the three girls, Charlotte, Emma, and Maggot, and by Jammy Hat.

# 8

They had planned their tournament for the next day. But as it turned out this was impossible. Some parents had roused that night in the village and discovered the children gone. They turned to the police, and now the whole school was in disgrace, suffering punishments varied according to grown-up whim. Marly and Bandy were made to work for their lives in the meat trade; Totty and Annie Feather's mother, though she did not mind what they did even at night, objected to policemen knocking at 2 A.M., and she showed her wrath by making the two eldest children do such jobs as washing nappies and chopping wood till they wanted to drop. Jammy and Scooter were soundly spanked and compared bruises for days after, forgetting that they were supposed to be deadly enemies. Ginger too was beaten by his redheaded father, and Molly was sent to bed early for a week without supper. Charlotte and Emma were shouted at for an hour by their angry grandfather Elijah, who threatened them with astrological spankings, though luckily this was only a threat; but they were told that they might not leave Aviary Hall for a week, nor have any of their friends to see them. This could not prevent the invisible coming of the boy, but Charlotte and Emma were gloomy at their new imprisonment and cross with one another most of the time.

Miss Gozzling scolded them for their crossness. The punishment was their own fault she said; she would have no sympathy with them, which was true because she too had been badly scolded by Grandfather Elijah for letting Charlotte and Emma run wild. Only old Bomble, the gardener, comforted them, said they were naughty little misses but nice, and he liked to see spirit in them he did, it were right they weren't allus good; so they went and talked to him, while he dug over the beds where the strawberries had passed, and sometimes were even allowed to play with the bantams from under his basket chair, whose wings were clipped like theirs that week so they could not fly where they wanted.

Only Maggot whose uncle did not mind what she did and Baby who had slept, escaped the general disgrace. Baby's mother gave him even more sweets than usual and was smug when the other parents discussed the matter in the village shop. Baby himself, who had grown nicer since he had learned to fly, was not smug; in fact, he was cross that he had not been woken and crosser still when Jammy told him he slept too soundly. And he was very cross with his mother, though he did not refuse the sweets, because he could not persuade her to let the other children watch their television all that week. But worse than the punishments and the disgrace, far worse than the denial of the television set, worse than anything for the children, were the new suspicions that their parents had.

'What could they have been doing on the Downs at midnight?' The question went back and forth in the village. The children hardly dared to make single leaps into the air in case the secret ceased to be a secret any more. It was decided by general agreement, relayed by the boy from house to house, that flying would have to cease for a while, and that the tournament must wait.

But by the time a week had passed, seaside holidays

78

had started. One by one the children went from the village. First Baby, whose holidays were always furthest and longest; then Molly, who went to a smart hotel in a smart seaside town with a promenade. Then Ginger was taken as usual to Margate. Then Mrs Feather took all her eight untidy children, including Totty and Annie, in a caravan to camp uncomfortably on a beach, and Scooter's and Jammy's parents removed Scooter and Jammy to a fishing village where fishermen wore navy blue jerseys and smoked pipes. Marly and Bandy did not go away, but they had to do all the work of their father's helpers who did; thus they had no time for flying. That left the boy, Maggot Hobbin, and Charlotte and Emma, who were never taken for holidays by the sea. This usually made them sad, but this year they did not mind; in fact, they were glad, for four of them on the same side could not make a tournament. So now it was their summer, their secret. They might enjoy it as they wanted, free of quarrels.

One day they themselves flew to the sea, to the glimmering through the Downs. Over the round hills they flew, over the rows of boarding houses down to the yellow sands and the weed-yellow rocks, to the endless sucking surge of the sea itself. They landed on an empty beach behind a headland and ran along it wildly, shoes, socks cast off, long hair streaming behind them. In the delights they found they almost forgot about flying. They poked about among uncovered rocks, dragged out reluctant crabs, and then let them go again to scuttle sideways on the wet sand. They slipped on damp rocks and lay full length to explore rock pools.

Presently Charlotte, who loved the sea specially, wandered off by herself. She lay on a flat sun-covered rock and watched the waves moving in. She watched one rock absorbedly, knowing its fate in the rising tide, but wishing, hoping, that it would escape the moving sea; because suddenly it seemed to her like their summer, which slipped away beneath quarrels and holidays and the moving year.

But the waves rose higher, green with white edges, and a curly tongue probed the shoulder of the rock to fall back sighing in a hollow. And a wave soon heaved above it, and water dribbled weakly down the landward side; and then waves rose higher and higher, not dribbling but pouring, surging over and over and over. At last the sea was smooth where the rock had been. Occasionally brown seaweed showed when the water slid apart, but soon even that was gone, as soon, thought Charlotte, soon, soon, the summer would be gone too.

She stood up carefully on her flat rock. She threw a pebble into the glittering sea and turned away back over the rocks to the beach where the others were building a sandcastle with shells for turrets.

She was sad after her thoughts, but she loved sand-castles, so now she made another beside them in competition and forgot her sadness in scratching out windows and moulding towers. She stuck different coloured seaweeds, fluffy ones, severe ones, to make a garden, and scooping out the wet, grainy sand with her fingers, made a moat, which the tide would fill as it came in. She worked absorbedly, and after a while the boy, not scornful as some boys would have been about sand-castles, came to help her, and they crouched silent over it on the sand with the sun hot on their backs.

The boy's cockleshell was hidden under a layer of freckle-coloured sand, which clung to his face and hair. Charlotte too had her layer of it where she had brushed away the hair from her eyes with a sand-covered hand.

She could feel it dried on her skin, and she was happy again. It was the sea, she thought, made her feel like this. It delighted her even more than wood or Downs; she felt it belonged to her and she to it. Perhaps that was because her father had been a sailor and she was said to be like him. Certainly the sea belonged to her more than to Maggot, whose brownness was of wood not sea, more than to Emma, who hated wet feet. It belonged to the boy too. In their feeling for the sea, he and Charlotte were fast friends, making a sandcastle together.

Emma was jealous. When she heard them talking about the sea, she told Charlotte that she was silly, that she worshipped the sea as if it were a god as they did in the very olden days, and that was silly.

'Why not go and be a shrimp in the sea if you like it so much?' she said and giggled. 'Or a lobster going all red as you're going now?' she added and giggled some more.

'Lobsters aren't red! They're blue,' said the boy firmly.

'Nonsense!' cried Emma, giggling still. 'They're red.'

'They're blue.'

'No, I don't believe you.' Emma became obstinate. 'They're red—'

'They're blue—'

'Not when Grandfather has them.'

'But that's when they're cooked,' said Charlotte, peacemaking as usual. But the boy had gone, flying out to the end of the rocks where the water was deep. He plunged like a gull beneath the sea and reappeared as suddenly, waving a monster, a space-age thing with wicked claws and a jointed writhing body plated in blue-green. He waved this triumphantly in front of the shrinking Emma.

'See, Miss?' he asked, angrily. 'Now do you believe

81

me?' But Emma would not admit herself wrong.

'No,' she said. 'That's not a lobster; that's different.'

'Don't be silly,' said the boy scornfully.

'No, I'm not,' cried Emma. 'It's not a lobster; I know it isn't.' She was almost tearful now and very determined, and it was lucky that Charlotte knew a way to curb Emma's temper, because the boy, on edge since the Totty quarrel, was growing angry in his teasing and waving the wicked claws dangerously close to Emma's nose.

'Don't you *dare* laugh, Emma,' said Charlotte warningly to her sister. 'Don't you dare laugh.' Emma bit her lip, but her face remained angry.

'I won't. I'm right, I *know*,' she said and stamped her foot, though that did not sound very good on sand. But she could not keep up her pretence after all and in the silence burst out laughing. The boy did the same.

'Anyway,' said Emma at last, 'its feelers are red,' and that was true. The antennae waving from the monster's head were bright scarlet.

# 9

The four children walked happily down the beach
together, watching the gulls skimming the waves. They
dropped sheer down from the cliff jutting above them
and dodged among the crests of the rising waves.

'I would like to do that,' said Charlotte to the boy,
quite serious.

'We can,' he answered her, 'but it's hard . . . Will you
try?'

Emma said hurriedly, looking at the great fall from the
cliff, 'I think I'm going to look for shells.' And Charlotte
too was frightened. It was not usually she who thought of
doing such things; usually it was the gymnasts such as
Marly and Bandy. But they were not here now. The sea
was fierce and active, swelling forth and back, and the
rocks were jagged. But still she wanted it.

'Yes, I'll try,' she said, looking at the boy, wide-eyed.

Maggot gave Charlotte a wise look. 'Yes,' she said,
'you should try; it's your place. But it's not mine, not
now. Come on, Emma, we'll find shells,' and they went
back up the beach, searching, bent over the ground.

'They won't find much with the tide this high,' said the
boy, looking back after them. Then he smiled at
Charlotte.

'Are you frightened?' he asked. But he was not
mocking her as he might have been, nor did he wait for an
answer.

They flew to the top of the cliff, and it was a hard flight, like a climb steeply upward, pushing with feet and hands while the face of the cliff fell below them. At the top Charlotte collapsed, exhausted, on the short springy grass and lay panting.

'Come on,' said the boy. 'Soon there will be no time.' So she went with him to the edge of the cliff, where the heather fell away and there was only rock. You could not fall far from here, for just below them a wide ledge jutted out. It was from this that the gulls fell like stones to the sea. Some of them sat motionless now; and all over the ledge were traces of others, draggled feathers and white stains.

The gulls were surprisingly tame. At least they made no move away from the two watching them. Charlotte felt that the boy was so familiar to them, they had no need to fear. All that they showed now was interest; smooth, rounded shapes hunched on match-stick legs, they swivelled their heads back to front to pin the two with beady eyes and pointed greedy beaks.

The boy nodded to Charlotte to stay on the cliff top and himself dropped down onto the ledge where the gulls were. He spoke to them in his soundless language, and they heard him, beady-eyed and motionless. 'Come,' said the boy upward, to Charlotte. Then she too slithered down to the gull rock. 'Come,' he said again and drew her to the edge. The cliff fell away to the sea, down and down to the moving water, where waves appeared wrinkles on a contour map and the toothy rocks harmless stones, waiting to be skimmed across the water like pebbles from a beach.

Charlotte's stomach did not seem to belong to her. The wind dragged back her hair and scoured her face, and in her ears was the sigh of the distant sea and the trickle of a tiny stream, which fell from the top to the bottom of the cliff.

'Come,' said the boy gently. 'You do want to come?' he asked anxiously, as she stood, silent and frightened, looking at the space lined by sea.

Charlotte, at that moment, did not want to go in the least, but she could not disappoint him now, hearing the anxiety in his voice. She looked up, not smiling, and said, 'Yes, but how?'

The boy said, 'The gulls will show us; I have asked them. We must watch what they do, and when they halt their fall, we must halt ours. They will halt it a little before they usually do, because we are larger and you are inexperienced, and then you must swerve immediately into the waves. Can you do it, do you think?'

Charlotte said, her stomach turning inside out, 'Is it dangerous?' The boy looked at her. His face was beaked and stern.

'The first time,' he said, 'yes. You could misjudge it, and then . . . perhaps I shouldn't ask you to come, Charlotte. I had forgotten a little what it was like.' Yet he was furiously anxious that she would not come. She could not bear to disappoint him: half of her anyway dragged to go, even if the other half, the timid flesh-half, dragged back.

'I am coming,' she said, her voice rising sharply. 'Let's go,' she added, trying to be carefree, though all of her trembled.

'Yes then, we go,' said the boy, smiling at her his best and unmocking smile. She was so delighted by this that she almost stepped straight off the cliff without thinking any more. But the boy caught her back.

'Wait for the gulls,' he said. He beckoned, and they jerked forward on slender legs to stand beside them on the cliff edge. Charlotte now was conscious of nothing but fear seizing her, cold, shivering, icy fear. The wind caught her skirt, her hair; hard rock was still beneath her feet. And then suddenly, almost unaware, she had left the rock and was plummeting, boy, birds with her, plummeting stonelike seaward in a rush of air.

It wasn't mere falling. She had to use some of her powers of flight to make it a controlled and not a helpless fall. Even so, she went so fast that she could hardly sense the speed except by the great pressure on her ears as she went down. The wind was wholly in her; her body belonged to it. There were only her thoughts left, falling from a cliff. She forgot everything, even the boy. Though her ears hurt more and more, she felt as if her head would burst like a balloon, she ignored it, thought only of this ecstasy—on and on and on.

But there was sound, wind-caught, somewhere. She looked round in an ease of movement that came once the first fear had gone. 'Stop! stop!' came the noise. Suddenly she realized that it was the boy, frantic, moving his hands at her down to the rushing sea. It was very near, leaping to meet her; and the gulls had stopped, swerved up. She was frightened again. But she jerked her whole body like a brake, jarred it through and through, and hovered, trembling level. But the sea, the rocks, rushed up no more. She had stopped just in time, a few feet above the jagged rock teeth that formed a chain from the cliff, like a necklace, more dangerous than diamonds.

All of her ached; numbly she followed the boy among the waves and dodged in them, her arms stretched out like wings splattered by the salt spray, feeding on wind and salt, turning into a trough and rising just in time to skim the crest of the next sea-green wave. That was exciting too; but not so good as that ear-pressed fall. Nothing would ever be as good as that. Not even the next fall, when she tried again to act as a gull, not even that was as good; though this time she remembered to stop and slid from fall to flight without jarring. Nothing would ever be like that first drop to the sea—down like a gull falling seaward from the cliff. It had been the best, yet somehow the saddest, happening of her whole life, but she could explain neither the happiness nor the sadness.

Meanwhile as she dodged among the waves, the boy and the gulls came on a shoal of little leaping fish and dived, greedily, swallowing them whole as they caught them. But the thought of the raw fish sickened Charlotte. Silently she dodged as the gulls screamed around her. What fishwives they sounded, what vulgar birds; yet it was they owned this pure falling from a cliff down to the surging sea, their white bodies streamlined as motors.

Even after they left the sea and went to find the others, Charlotte remained silent. Emma bubbled with questions: 'What was it like? Was it frightening? Could I have come too? In fact I wish I had now; it looked super.' But Charlotte answered her only briefly. Sometimes a longing to talk about the fall came over her, but when she opened her mouth to try and explain, someone was sure to say, 'Oh, look at those fishes,' or, 'The gulls are making an awful lot of noise now,' things that had no part in what she wanted to say and that stopped her being able to say them.

Emma's questions ceased quite soon. Maggot had never even asked any. She looked at Charlotte, brown-eyed, and Charlotte knew that Maggot understood without words what she could not explain. So did the boy. He hardly talked to her again that day. But sometimes he smiled, his nicest unmocking smile, the cockleshell freckles stretched wide on his face.

# 10

Soon after this the rest of the school came drifting back to the village from their holidays. But Charlotte was still dazed by joy and lived through the discussions, the meetings, and the plannings that took place about the battle in a dream. Only the night before did she wake up to the fact that the battle was serious, that if the boy's side did not win, he would leave the very next day. They might know the secret of his coming, but that would not make up for the fact of his going. So she lay awake half the night in sick anticipation, watching the moon, uncaring, outside the window and reliving the whole summer in her mind.

Every now and then she imagined the next day vividly. She imagined the triumph if they won, heard the voices of each of them and the things they would say. Then she imagined failure; how unbearable, how terrible that would be! She could hear the boy saying goodbye, the children's answers. The pain bit into her; she ached with it, even wept into her pillow until it was damp, in the misery of the possibility. Then she told herself she was being silly and fell asleep at last to dream yet more vividly of the next day; the boy like an eagle, clawed and beaked, terrible in the sky; and her own tears, dropping huge and hot, down to burned downland earth where they turned into whole nestfuls of baby gulls with staring scarlet eyes.

She woke suddenly, thinking it must be very late, for it was so in her dream. But there was no noise in the house.

The sun fell weakly through the window; it was the early-morning sunlight of a perfect September day, and it meant that she had a long time to lie awake.

The sick feeling came back to her stomach. She almost woke Emma, leaning over to prod the blanketed hump that was her sister, before deciding that she could not explain even to Emma quite what this fight could mean to her. So she lay, eyes wide, staring at the ceiling, and tried unsuccessfully to forget about it.

The children had argued in a long meeting the day before how everything was to be arranged. They had decided on 'French and English' as the basis of their battle rules, since they all knew it and it would not have to be explained many times over to the stupidest among them, such as Molly Scobb and Baby Fumpkins. But it was to be played, obviously, flying.

The place they chose for fighting was more like a battlefield than a playground. About two miles from the village lay a dip in the Downs, quite high up. Apart from a dew pond right in the centre at its lowest point, the ground was bare, but on either side of the dip small, rather straggly beechwoods clung to the slopes. These woods were to be the opposing camps. From their trees would dangle the flags—seven for each side—which the girls had made from handkerchiefs, with crested badges sewn on them, an eagle on red for the boy's side, an owl on blue for Totty's. That had been Emma's idea, to make the battle more real. To lose all the flags would be to lose the battle.

Any of the children might try to steal the enemy flags, but any of them caught on the enemy side of the dew pond would be prisoners until they were rescued by a fellow knight: for they were to be called knights, they decided eagerly, except for Jammy and Scooter, who could only be squires because they were so small. All of them, especially Charlotte, who had read many books, wanted to make it as much like a battle in olden days as possible. So they decided that, as well as the flags, they would have Supply Trains, the baggage to consist of sweets, and everyone agreed to give up their weekly allowance to buy it. Each side's supply would be placed in a tree like the flags. To lose it would be to lose greatly—half their crested pennants and half their prisoners.

They had become so excited about the plans that they nearly forgot they were supposed to be deadly enemies. Indeed, throughout the meetings and arguments they were very friendly. Disagreement over details arose just as much between members of the same side as between members of the different sides, and the feeling of rancour that had been in the air before the holidays seemed to have died out, which was strange now they were preparing for the battle it had caused. Yet there was no thought in any mind that they should abandon the battle, and it was lucky that they could be quite friendly in deciding the rules and the place for the fighting.

They gathered by the dew pond at the centre of the hollow on a morning as glowing and unconcerned as any other summer day. But they were more silent and shy as they had been when first they flew, though now they were practised flyers, clever as footballers at darting and turning and feinting. They all had a sick feeling in their stomachs, a school-examination feeling.

'Perhaps we'd better start,' said Totty briskly, but with a catch in his voice that was nervousness not tears. 'Should we toss for sides?' he asked, turning to the boy. But none of them had any pennies, so they had to use lengths of grass, thin and flat, which Charlotte held carefully in her closed hand. Totty won and chose his camp. There was little difference between the two woods, but his winning seemed an omen, and the boy's side was gloomy.

They ranged themselves in line and waited. It seemed endless, the time of silent waiting, but suddenly they had begun almost without realizing it. And in the rushings of air and the shoutings and the handkerchief wavings it seemed impossible that silence and waiting could ever have existed.

# 11

Soon—out of the flurry of trying and seizing and failing, catching and being caught, diving down from the air, shooting up like planes and grabbing the unwary—a pattern emerged, encouraged by whispered orders from Totty and the boy to their knights and little squires. On Totty's side Marly and Bandy and Totty himself were the chief flag snatchers and managed to avoid capture surprisingly easily, despite the swiftness of Maggot and the boy, skimming unexpected in the air. On the other side the boy was the main attacker. He could be in twenty places at once, or so it seemed, taking back a flag, rescuing a prisoner (it was invariably Jammy), defeating the efforts of the other side to seize their pennants. Maggot was swift, but not as swift as he. Ginger flew far slower than either, but his solidity made him a formidable defender, too formidable for such as Annie Feather and Molly Scobb, too formidable even for Scooter Dimple, though not for the Scraggs, who made him look like a sky whale faced by sky porpoises. He could not catch them in long flight; he could not catch them at all, which was probably why, when they came to the first pause they had agreed to have in the battle, they saw that Totty's side was piling up flags and prisoners far too quickly.

Breathing heavily, hair over their eyes, legs scratched red from beech twigs, they glared at each other across the pond, real enmity entering into their battle. Scooter

Dimple stuck out his tongue at Jammy Hat and said, 'Yah', which was not very subtle but effective.

When the battle began again, Jammy forgot the order that he was to defend only. He charged across to Totty's territory and was pursued by Scooter. Breathlessly they dodged each other above the dew pond. Scooter nearly put a hand on Jammy's rubbed corduroy shorts. He missed; he tried again, snatching desperately; and this time he seized them hard and pulled Jammy. They both fell into the pond with an outrush of wild water. It was just like the day at the lake, only now it was not funny. No one laughed. It was not a holiday now; it was a battle and fighting they almost hated each other. Jammy was a prisoner, wet and shivering in Totty's prison camp; so was Emma, caught by Molly and Annie combined; so was Charlotte; so was Ginger after one of his rare ventures over the enemy lines, though he managed to free Jammy. As well as Charlotte, Emma, and Ginger, Totty's side held ten of the fourteen flags, six of their own, four of the boy's. As for the boy, all he had were four handkerchief-made flags with emblems of owl and eagle, and one useless prisoner, Baby Fumpkins, who was slow and panted like an old dog.

They paused, breathless, wondering what they should do next, what could happen now. Totty, triumphant, harangued his followers to victory. But the boy was very grave. He put Jammy to defend the supply tree, as that would be in danger now that three were prisoners. He himself set out grimly to attack, while Maggot hovered behind him, six feet above the dew pond, to protect the camp from other onslaughts. It was a slender barrier, only herself against six of the other side.

Scooter passed Maggot easily to rescue Baby. The two of them saw Jammy guarding the supply tree, content to be there. They saw him guiltily take a peppermint, look round to see if anyone was looking, and push it hastily into his mouth. There was a smell of peppermint, a very strong smell, and the sound of Jammy loudly sucking.

Scooter and Baby looked at one another.

'If we get the supplies . . .' said Scooter.

'We might win . . .' said Baby.

'And of course it wouldn't matter if we had one or two sweets . . .'

'It would be a fair reward,' decided Baby.

'So let's try,' cried Scooter. They charged Jammy. But it was not so easy as that. While Jammy sat in front of the sweets, they were his, and he had only to touch his enemies' clothes for them to be prisoners again. So they dodged about and tried to lure him away by insults.

'Greedy,' said Scooter.

'Who's stealing?' called Baby.

'Fat face,' cried Scooter.

'Thief,' shouted Baby.

Jammy got very red in the face. Any minute he might leap on them, and then one of them would seize the supply, and that would nearly be that. But still Jammy sat on the tree limb, swinging his legs.

Their shouting was heard over the battlefield, heard by Annie Feather and Molly Scobb, who were very curious and, when they saw what the commotion was about, very greedy.

'Shouldn't we help?' said Annie.

'Perhaps we could,' said Molly.

'I'm hungry.' Annie sighed.

'So am I,' sighed Molly. They looked round to see if they could take any of their own supplies, but there was Totty glaring, so hastily they withdrew their eyes.

'Maggot couldn't catch both of us,' declared Annie.

'And we're winning by miles,' cried Molly, as they too went chasing over the battlefield. By now there was such a noise from the boy's supply tree that even Bandy's and Marly's attention was drawn for a while. As for Totty, he was skirmishing with Maggot above the dew pond, each trying to lure the other to capture. For the moment, Totty's supply tree was unwatched except by the prisoners, Charlotte, Ginger, and Emma.

Desperately they willed the boy to see and come, see and come. Could he, would he? It seemed so easy, so obvious from here, but he had a whole battlefield to watch. Yet suddenly he saw and he came, swift in the air to seize the supplies and bear them easily home, with Marly and Bandy, warned, too late, useless on his tail, while Charlotte cheered and shouted.

And at last there was only one flag left on Totty's side, a flag with an owl on it. Totty appointed himself chief protector of this, the one flag left to him. He crossed his arms and spread his legs in the air. He stood there, guarding with his life.

And the boy came. He did not need to dodge the others. They looked at his face and drew aside in awe. It was fierce, his face, fierce and beaked; he was an eagle. Totty was only a wagtail, but he stayed unmoving and watched the boy come, watched him until they were face to face, beak to beak, glaring. Then they were fighting in the air, and the others knew it was inevitable. Whoever won this fight would win the battle, whatever had happened before. It had to be; Charlotte knew it now. The boy had to fight his own battle, Totty his. They fought, one to win the solitary flag, the other to keep it. They fought.

It was even, surprisingly so. They dodged in mid-air like animals, like a bull and a bullfighter, Totty the bull, although he was small, the boy elegant, the master, moving little, swinging his body out of the way as Totty charged head down to catch him. But they did not hit each other, according to the rules. For minutes, for an age, they circled, feinted, dodged evenly.

They were getting tired. Totty's glasses were long since lost. His black hair fell over his eyes. He panted. But the boy was almost worse. His delicate birdlike body seemed ready to break. He was growing desperate. He swerved again, a hopeless swerve. Totty darted after, while Charlotte watched, shaking with apprehension. But the boy, gathering strength, suddenly sprang. Totty sprang after him, but too late—the flag was in the boy's hand. In the desperation of tiredness the boy shot straight below Totty, a gull movement, and escaped him. There was the dew pond; there was the halfway line; there was Totty still chasing. And there was home and safety at last. The battle was over; the boy had won.

# PART THREE

# 1

The time that followed the battle was the children's glorious summer. The days were golden, blue days, days that began greyly in mist and grew slowly to colour as the morning strengthened. Autumn things ripened, hips and haws, blackberries sweet and sour, and chestnut burrs from the trees that guarded the schoolyard. At first they were green and damp, and when the children stamped on them, milk-white nuts rolled out. But as September passed, the husks hardened, grew browner and pricklier, and the nuts inside swelled huge and rich and red. The children went mad under the chestnut trees by the railings, grabbing nuts from the grass and playing conkers with them like champions. Mad children they were, bird children, for this year the best nuts did not stay on the topmost branches, safe from the stones thrown to knock them down. The children, flying, brought them to earth triumphant over the tallness of the trees. It was the same with everything, high-growing blackberries, high-growing cobnuts—all came easily to their hands as they flew. But once picked, nothing was quite as huge as it looked from ground level, Charlotte reflected, surveying a smallish chestnut that had seemed a colossus.

They flew on long explorings everywhere. It was wonderful, extraordinary, what they had wanted all summer. But just as the chestnuts ripened, time went by until there were only six days, then five, then four, then three, then two till term began.

They met sadly on that second to last day. They did not know how to spend the precious day left to them; it had to be so special. Tomorrow, tomorrow, tomorrow; afterwards it would be all different, they knew, all finished.

The boy was very strange that morning, silent and looking at them sideways from chestnut eyes. He was on edge too. Charlotte felt that she understood him less than she had ever done. 'What do you think we should do?' she asked him to try and make him come alive again.

He did not answer her at first. They waited anxiously for his reply, even Totty, who, the battle lost and over, had accepted the boy's leadership without fuss almost as if he had been tired of the differences himself. At last the boy spoke, and because of what he said, they met next day to fly to the lake, puzzled and curious because they had sensed in his suggestion something hidden, something he would not tell.

They flew over the parkland and the changing trees to the lake where Old Moo presided with her broken nose and her rakish ivy crown. Leaves floated on the water beneath the little temple. It looked forlorn today, broken, under skies that for the first time in weeks were grey, and with a wind that had almost a winter chill to it. Charlotte and Emma had been forced to wear raincoats by Miss Gozzling. They had not argued much, in case she spoiled their day, but they had taken them off immediately upon leaving Aviary Hall as a sign of rebellion, although the coats were a nuisance to carry and they were cold enough to need them. The other children had got away without trouble, parents having forgotten by now the night of the moon picnic; all except Jammy Hat, who was locked in his bedroom for cheeking his father but who had flown unrepentant out of the window.

Now they gathered by the lake. The brambles were crowded with blackberries, and they ate before they took council, cramming purple berries greedily to their mouths till their hands and lips were stained.

But the boy stood sternly beneath Old Moo and waited for them to stop eating and keep silence. He seemed more like a bird than ever today. His limbs were more stretched and angled, his nose longer. His cockleshell was plain, his eyes very bright, and he ate insects unceasingly, like a child let loose in a sweet shop.

'This is my day,' he said at last, 'this is my day,' and they did not question it but waited.

'As it is my day,' he said, 'I want all of you to come with me. I've got a place, a special place. I want to show it to you. Will you come?'

'Yes,' they said, awed by him. 'Is it far? Should we come?'

'Please come,' he answered persuasively, his face glowing with joy. 'I want you to, all of you. You won't regret it, I know.'

'But what's it like?' said practical Totty. 'Will it take long to get there? Will we be back by teatime? My mum said she'd tan the hide off me if I wasn't back by then.'

'But everything's all right,' insisted the boy. 'I promise.' He was on edge, excited and jerky. Charlotte watched him closely. A leaf floated down on his head and poised there like a crest, but he did not notice it.

'Come with me, come with me, come with me,' he crooned, hypnotic, and 'Let's go!' they cried, stirred by him. They gathered strength for flight, grouped on the steps beneath Old Moo. But Charlotte knew something was wrong. She could not go; she could not let the others go with such a sense of suspicion in her. Yet they were all fired by the boy's enthusiasm, even silly Molly and solid

Annie; and Emma was alight with it, clasping her navy blue raincoat to her.

Charlotte tried to catch the boy's eye, but he would not look at her. That was unusual too. The children rose in the air, the boy urging them on. There was excitement at the mystery, a chatter like starlings. But Charlotte took her courage and spoke out clearly above it.

'Where are we going?' she asked sternly.

'My secret!' cried the boy, mocking her as he had not mocked her for many days, not since that gull plunge from the cliff.

'No,' she said. 'No; *our* secret. Where are you taking us? I want to know.'

'And I,' said the boy, 'I don't want to tell you.'

'Shut up, Charlotte,' the rest said, impatiently hovering, urging flight. 'We want to go. It doesn't matter—he won't take us anywhere bad.'

'NO,' said Charlotte again, obstinately. 'I want to know. I won't go until I do.' She knew as she said this that it was only herself against them all, that they had only to fly off and she would be helpless. Indeed, she would go with them; she would not bear being left behind. It was hard to hide this before the staring eyes of the others.

'Charlotte, Charlotte, Charlotte,' they seemed to be muttering, strangers suddenly turned against her. The boy played to it.

'You trust me, all of you,' he appealed, 'don't you?' His chestnut eyes looked anxious. He mocked Charlotte. Yet she became aware that he was desperate, so she said more gently as he hovered in the air before her:

'Tell me—where are you taking us?'

But he ignored her. Charlotte was almost crying. All eyes looked at her; all eyes, even Emma's. Only Maggot, her friend, was aloof, looking out over the lake; otherwise it was all eyes. Very sternly, in a last effort, Charlotte said:

'None of us are coming unless you tell us where we are going, none of us.' And she looked at the boy straight, forcing his eyes up to hers. The mockery quivered and was suddenly gone. He brushed his hair back and with it the leaf that had fallen on his head an age before and looked at her beseechingly for a moment. Then he fell to the ground stricken and crouched there shaking, his arm curved above his head like a protective wing. He was weeping, and quivering all over like a bird caught in a trap. Charlotte was ashamed and landed swiftly beside him to stroke and soothe him while he wept. The children hovering over were a bodyguard; and Maggot was an angel, watching and determined.

At last the boy looked up, no longer tearful.

'Charlotte's right,' he said. 'I don't think you would regret coming with me. You'd be children for ever. You'd fly for ever. But I must tell you this. You could never come back.'

# 2

The children were awed. They talked among themselves. 'Couldn't we still go?' asked Totty.

'Yes, yes, yes,' came the chorus from Marly and Bandy Scragg, who hated butcher's chores.

'Could I go and not have to face my mum?' asked Jammy, who had escaped from a window.

'No more Miss Gozzling!' cried Emma. Now Charlotte had a new form of opposition to face, and a worse one in that she herself longed to go. No more yew trees, no more Miss Gozzling. There would be the sea and flying, and the boy for ever and ever and ever. Yet she knew that it must not be. She remembered the poem of the piper who charmed the children away and the parents' grief. They could not go, not all of them; yet her longing to go ached inside her.

She had allies in her decision. Annie Feather and Molly Scobb said firmly, or rather Annie did but Molly always followed, 'We're staying here,' for they could not imagine or want another life than the life they had in the village. Charlotte was not sure that their help was not more of a hindrance; the school never liked to agree with the solid things said by Annie, echoed by Molly.

The children were excited and whispering, the boy, a draggled bird, was looking at her beseechingly with new hope in his eyes, so that she could scarcely bear to meet his gaze.

Emma said, 'Don't be a spoilsport, Char. Don't say we

mustn't.'

But Charlotte's voice came out of herself in agony, because there was only herself, unwilling and slight, between their going and their staying.

'But think, think . . .'

'Think what?' said Totty rudely. 'Don't you think it'd be better to spend our lives flyin' than growin' up and goin' to work at eight o'clock every day? No more work, no nothin': just doin' what we like all day. Wouldn't that be better, stupid Char?'

'Don't talk to her like that—let her speak her turn,' cried the boy fiercely. 'Speak, Charlotte,' he added to her surprise, almost gently. But she did not know what to say.

'Listen, everyone,' she said slowly at last. 'You see—if we go—what's left?'

'All my brothers and sisters,' said Totty. The school laughed. Charlotte went red.

'No, shut up, Totty,' came her voice surprisingly to the once leader. 'No, but if we go, what will our families say, our mothers and fathers? They'll worry dreadfully . . . And would we really never want to see anyone again?' went on Charlotte. 'Haven't you ever been homesick, any of you?'

'No,' said Bandy Scragg. But some of the others had; she could see by their faces.

'What about Grandfather Elijah—wouldn't he mind? And wouldn't you miss him?' said Charlotte to Emma. 'And what about your mothers; would you never want to see them again?'

'I'd miss my mum,' came from Baby Fumpkins.

'But I'm feared what my mum will say now,' wailed Jammy.

'Listen,' went on Charlotte, 'and think of them, all of

you, how miserable they'd be. And Miss Hallibutt, she wouldn't have any teaching, she wouldn't have any money any more.' They liked Miss Hallibutt since the day of her discovery; she was a person too, and they would be sorry to harm her.

But still Charlotte knew she had failed; yet it mattered so much that they should stay; she did not know quite why. She put her head in her hands, despairingly.

The boy looked at her; he looked at all of them gathered on the ground, on the overgrown steps by the grey lake. Then he flew to the top of the temple and leaned on the ivy-clad head of Old Moo watching them, brooding, very still. He spoke.

'Charlotte is right,' he said. 'I shan't let any of you come. You must not. It would be bad. I should be a thief stealing lives.'

But his eyes were dark, lustreless like chestnuts kept in a box.

Charlotte flew to comfort him. Then he said: 'I wanted you to come, Charlotte,' and she longed to cry but could not in front of all of them, especially as they were cross because the boy had forbidden their coming and they thought it was Charlotte's fault.

'An' I've gotter see my mum *and* my dad,' wailed Jammy.

Maggot had been aloof all the time, watching a piece of weed moving on the lake. But now she turned and looked at them. 'You cannot go,' she said gently. 'But I must go. I have no reason to stay.'

Charlotte knew that Maggot was right, and Maggot was her friend; but she was jealous.

So on the Downs that evening they said goodbye—to the boy, with him the lean brown Maggot, and to the power of flight.

The boy lingered behind with Charlotte while the others moved on. He did not say much to her; only his smile was there, unmocking.

Charlotte said, 'I shan't ever forget.'

'No,' said the boy.

'I don't know why I stopped us coming. I didn't want to. I'm sorry; but I had to, you see. I don't know why.'

'I know,' said the boy. 'I know.'

'And Maggot? Are you happy she's coming with you?'

'Yes,' said the boy. 'Maggot is my friend. But it would have been good if you could have come, Charlotte.'

'Oh,' said Charlotte, 'would it?' though he had spoken very like that in the morning. But she needed to hear it again now as he was going.

'Yes,' said the boy. 'I mean it, stupid. Did you think I didn't?' and he was mocking again and flew on to the others, looking back over his shoulder at her, his freckles stretched wide.

And then they were gone, he and Maggot, over the hills to the sea, like great birds in the distance. The children had not imagined properly what it would mean to have the boy gone, not even Charlotte. Now they knew or half knew, for the strangeness was still too great and too new for them to understand it fully. They stood on the Downs, numb and wind-blown, looking down towards the village.

Suddenly the rain came, beating in with the wind. At the same moment the sun shone out over the sea behind them, and one field below, the field by the school that had been yellow with buttercups in May, now was yellow with sun. A rainbow sprang vividly. A rainbow should be a hopeful thing, but it was not to them that day, especially not to Charlotte, caught in her own persuading and shunned for it, almost as she had been before the summer started and the children did not know her. 'Prig Charlotte'—the whispers were there again, Annie and Molly with the others, as the rain beat on their faces.

At the bottom of the Downs Miss Hallibutt met them in their flightless going. 'Hullo, children,' she cried. 'Ready for a new term?' They scowled at her and did not want to talk. Her smile fell away, and she looked sorry, so they were ashamed, remembering how nice she could be, and muttered, 'Yes, Miss Hallibutt,' and tried to smile. Then they dragged on, kicking at stones, while her eyes followed as if she knew what had happened and was sad for them.

At the end of the lane Charlotte and Emma said goodbye to the others, who did not smile, not even Ginger at Emma, and went slowly up the hill, truly on foot for the first time since May. Away from the village they went, away from the Downs and from the sea, up to Aviary Hall, to the humming-birds and the Roman bath, to their grandfather Elijah studying astrology, and Miss Gozzling who was idle; up to the yew trees in the garden, the kitchen-garden and greenhouses and Old Bomble the gardener, whose bantams under a bath chair could not fly, though the swallows could, wheeling across the lawn before their flight to the south. But there was nothing to remind Charlotte of the gull fall from the cliff down to the moving sea. The boy had gone.